The
Self-Esteem Workbook
for teens

A Highly Effective Guide To Help You Conquer Negative Thinking And Be Your Best Self.

Samantha Krimer

Blank Page

Blank Page

TABLE OF CONTENTS

Preface ____ 1

The Origin of Self-Hate____ 4

self-rejection____ 23

Substitutes for Love ____ 31

How Guilt, Embarrassment, and a Sense of Inferiority Create a Weak Self-image___________ 36

How to Tell If You Lack a Proper Self-Love _____________________ 50

Test To Determine The Degree Of Your Self-Acceptance _________ 74

What Self-Love Is Not____ 77

Benefits Of Self-Love ____ 97

how to rebuild your self-esteem _______________________________ 125

Conclusion____ 173

Bibliography____ 177

<u>PREFACE</u>

While it is relatively simple to name the steps by which one can achieve a greater degree of self-love (self-approval, a better self-image, self-acceptance, self-esteem), it is somewhat more difficult to apply these principles. Reading the formula will not suffice. One must work at it diligently and faithfully, and the task must be given priority.

In order to learn to like or love yourself, you must first find out who you are and how you became the person you are. Your name is not your identity. Nor is your role as mother, father, student, employee. You are much more than your role in life.

Many people believe that they know themselves well. Wet they seldom do.

We can never, now ourselves fully, but we can begin the process of discovering somewhat more completely who we are. Paradoxically, we come to know ourselves in the act of self-disclosure.

Talking about oneself in a narcissistic manner is not self-disclosure.

The true sharing of one's inner self can take place only in a setting where openness and honesty are encouraged, where there is no possibility of being judged or criticized.

The dialogue takes place best with a person or persons who will listen to, and affirm, the one sharing. Some sharing groups provide this opportunity.

A book, at best, can provide one with insights, stimulate one's thinking, and suggest a course of action.

It is very rare that the mere reading of a book and giving intellectual assent to some concepts has changed lives.

But reading books can bring new stimuli, open new vistas, and offer a new course of action.

The rest depends on the commitment a person put into the process.

Most of us are somewhat lazy or tend to procrastinate, Discipline, doing what we ought, when we should, whether we feel like it or not, is seldom easy.

" Life is like an onion. You take off one layer at a time, and sometimes you cry."

Carl Sandburg

THE ORIGIN OF SELF-HATE

From listening to many hundreds of primal experiences, we have learned that, though parents may love the child, if there are too little holding and cuddling and too much criticism and scolding, the child invariably feels,

'They don't like me. I am bad. I will do anything if they will only love me, but nothing works. They hate me. I am worthless. I hate myself."

We dislike ourselves because, in infancy and childhood, we experienced such feelings as these:

- *They don't want me.*
- *I'm no good.*
- *I'm not supposed to cry. It makes them angry when I cry.*
- *I'll be punished if I'm not quiet (good).*
- *They hate me.*
- *I hate myself*
- *It bothers them when I make a noise.*
- *They must never know what I'm feeling; it upsets them.*

- *If they hit me, I mustn't cry.*
- *They hate me unless I'm good (quiet).*
- *I hate myself because I can't always be good.*
- *I'm worthless; scared; lonely; guilty.*

These and scores of other feelings have been verbalized with intensity in thousands of hours of primal experiences
The pain relieved and expressed in tears, sobs, and screams reveal the reason adults so often hate themselves: they felt hated as infants and small children because they were not loved in a manner they could accept.
They felt unloved because they were not held, cuddled, touched, or because they were screamed at, beaten, scolded, and told in a hundred different ways that they were bad, a nuisance, stupid, wrong.

It is widely recognized that the child's personality is formed by the age of four or five, certainly by six. I did not know what enormous scars childhood Pain^ could leave until, in conducting In-Depth sessions with patients, I heard them relive their hurts hour by hour, hurt by hurt, scream by scream. The reliving of such traumas discharges the tension and anxiety encapsulating the childhood Pain.

It is largely because of early primal hurts that people dislike themselves. The harsh parental criticism, spoken or implied, becomes the child's conviction: "I am stupid." The parental expression of irritation or disgust becomes the child's feeling: "I'm no good. I irritate people."

Repression leads to obsession. In some cases, one can have repressed so much hurt and anger that his obsessive behavior became almost unendurable.

What is it that parents do to children that causes them to repress their true feelings? And how can children be allowed to express all of their "unacceptable feelings"? Let's take up the last question first.

HANDLING "UNACCEPTABLE" FEELINGS

We have three choices: To express feelings, which may or not be appropriate at a particular time; to suppress those feelings, meaning to be aware of them, but also to realize it is not appropriate to express them just then; or to repress them, bury them, deny that they exist, and then struggle to keep those "guilty," unacceptable feelings in the unconscious, at the cost of real damage to the personality.

Childhood hurts that we were not allowed to express simply added to the pool of primal Pain. It becomes "stored pain," which will ultimately express itself in emotional or physical symptoms.

The mother of a small child was embarrassed when her youngster began screaming in a store. He wanted a toy he saw on the counter. The mother didn't know just what to do, and, not wanting to spank him, allowed him to roll on the floor, screaming. A crowd gathered, and angry muttering was heard about what a rotten mother she was.

Embarrassed by the commotion and the criticism, she dragged the screaming child to the car and closed the windows. When he subsided, she said, *"Jimmy, I can understand your wanting that toy. It's okay to want it, but it's not all right to scream like that in public. People don't understand. Anytime you want to cry, let me know, and we will go off by ourselves, and you can cry all you need to."*

A few days later, having experienced a disappointment at home, he told his mother that he felt like crying. She said, *"All right, let's go into the bedroom and you can cry and be just as mad as you feel like."* He had a good cry, and when he finished, she hugged him. He was learning that crying was an all-right thing, in the right place. That is a vast improvement over the standard phrase, *"Stop crying (stop hurting), or I'll give you something to cry about!"*

Parental "Put-Downs" Do Permanent Damage

From hundreds of counselees, I had heard parent "put-downs," and I asked some of them to list the ones that they resented the most. I have selected some pertinent ones. These verbal put-downs, with fantasized responses, help explain how we got the way we are:

o I've told you a thousand times!

o What in the world are we going to do with you?

o Why do you do those stupid things?

o Oh, for heaven's sake!

o You know better than that!

o You should have been a boy.

o What did I ever do to deserve this?

o How many times have I told you?

o You'll never amount to a thing!

o Hold your shoulders back!

o Stand up straight!

o Can't you be more careful!

o What's the matter with you?

o Did you hear me?

o Don't bother me!

o Shut up!

o Why can't you grow up?

o Use your head!

o After all, I've done it for you!

o Don't you have any pride?

o You'll be the death of me yet.

o Go to your room till you're sorry.

o I'm disappointed in you!

o Money doesn't grow on trees.

o What makes you so stupid!

o You can do better than that!

o What did you do that for?

o Good grief, look what you did!

o I'm going to slap your face if you do that again!

o Why can't you be more like your sister (brother)?

o Why do you get into so much trouble?

o Why can't you be more like other boys?

o You make me sick!

o You're going to come to a bad end!

o   Stop biting your nails.

o   Don't be so silly.

o   You shouldn't/^f/ that way.

o   Can't you do anything right?

o   Would that please Jesus?

o   God can see you wherever you are!

o   God doesn't love naughty little girls.

o   What are you doing for heaven's sake?

o   How dumb can you get?

o   What will the neighbors say?

o   You owe it to us.

o   Keep quiet. Shut up.

o   You don't know what you're talking about.

o   Get out of my way!

o   Quit crying, or I'll slap you again!

o   Why don't you smile?

o   What a dumb thing to do!

o   I'm disappointed in you.

o   You're bad.

o   Hold your stomach in!

o Look at this room!

o Don't talk back to me!

o Why don't you say something? You never talk!

o Didn't you hear me when I called?

o Are you deaf?

o When will you stop being so clumsy?

The child's self-image is being formed in his early years. He either learns that he is loved, that he is a great kid, basically good, doing his best, and is going to succeed in life, or that he is not loved, but impatiently endured, that he is bad or stupid, and will probably come to a bad end

Parents can be driven beyond endurance by frustrating, irritating, exasperating children. They often feel a mixture of self-pity and anger that children can be so demanding, so unbelievably awful. It's not easy being a parent.

Try to avoid blaming your parents or yourself.

There is no one to blame. We are all trying to do our best nearly all the time. That our best is so often pitifully inadequate is simply part of the human condition. Call it original sin, corporate guilt, or human fallibility, it all adds up to the same thing

.

THE DOUBLE BIND

It is equally frustrating and damaging to put the child in a double bind. George, a delightful but unbelievably tense and anxious man of forty, said, "My mother kept asking me as a child why I didn't talk. I didn't know why, of course. She used to say, *'You never talk! What's the matter with you?'* I could only imagine that there was something wrong with me, but when I tried to say something, she would invariably jump down my throat, always showing me where I was wrong, or why I shouldn't feel the way I did. There was no way I could win with her."

A Fetus Is a Person, Who Feels!

Life begins, not just at birth, but before birth.

Unborn children can learn, feel pain, acquire likes and dislikes, and even become bored in the womb, according to Professor William Liley of Auckland University.

He stated in a lecture, "The process of learning to suck, to drink, to use one's lungs and limbs, begins in the womb, in one environment, in preparation for emergence into another environment at birth." He went on to say that "the unborn child is responsive to pain and touch, to cold and sound and light. He gets hiccups and sucks his thumb. He winks and sleeps. He gets bored with repetitive signals but can be taught to be alerted by a first signal or a different one." Sir William's conclusions were based on experiments with unborn children at Auckland University, New Zealand.

There is considerable evidence, too, that the unborn child feels very much what the mother feels. Her anxiety, or fear, happiness or depression, are felt by the child, since, after all, the child is still part of the mother.

Whether or not one is prepared to accept that without question, it is generally conceded that the first few years of life are of enormous importance.

We cannot be certain of all the forces that were brought to bear upon us in those earliest years since far more than nine-tenths of all that transpired from birth to age five has been buried, but what transpired in those early years formed us and made us what we are.

It is not only the verbal put-downs that damage a child. An unfeeling parent, unable to express love, can produce a child whose feelings are blocked; and the results range from anxiety, depression, and general ineffectiveness to mental illness.

Without knowing all of the details, we can sense the general outline: all of us, even in the most enlightened and loving home environment, were damaged to some extent; for as there are no perfect parents, there is no perfect environment, and thus there are no perfect children grown into adults.

We dislike ourselves in direct proportion to the amount of rejection and criticism we experienced in childhood. We like and accept ourselves to the degree that our parents loved and accepted us— in a manner we could accept.

Bland, unfeeling, nontouching parents produce children who tend to feel unworthy and self-rejecting.

They find it hard to accept compliments and experience an excessive amount of free-floating anxiety.

The infant who was not held or cuddled or affirmed will become an adult with deep anxiety, and physical or emotional problems.

We learn to love by having been loved.

Very often, an individual is limited in self-love because, as a child, there was little or no love shown. In the early part of this century, the school of "behaviorism" flourished for a time and had a great deal of damaging influence upon the children of those who followed behaviorist principles.

In order to understand the behaviorist school of thoughtfully, consider this statement by Dr. J. B. Watson, its founder:

Mothers just don't know; when they kiss their children and pick them up and rock them, caress them and jiggle them upon their knee, that they are slowly building up a human being totally unable to cope with the world, it must later live in. There is a sensible way of treating children. Treat them as still; they were young adults. Never hug or kiss them, never let them sit on your lap if you must kiss them on the forehead when they say goodnight. Can't a mother train herself to substitute a kindly word, a smile, in all her dealings with the child, for the kiss and the hug, the pickup, and the coddlings? ... If you haven't a nurse and cannot leave the child, put it out in the back yard, a large part of the day. Build a barrier around the grass so that you are certain no harm can come to it. Do this from the time it is born. If your heart is too kind and you must watch the child, make yourself an opening so that you can see it without being seen. Finally, learn not to talk in endearing and coddling terms.

Many parents who are horrified by such an approach to childrearing have done irreparable harm to their children by alternating between over permissiveness and punitiveness, by excessive criticism, and in a thousand other ways. Most of us, in fact, have been damaged to some extent, large or small, by well-meaning parents who firmly believed they loved us, yet who failed to display it in the simplest and most fundamental ways—by touching and cuddling, by praise and affirmation. Such people cannot like or love themselves, because they were not loved in a way they could readily accept. Parents often send a double message: the verbal message is "You know how much we love you, dear; just see all the things we do for you, and all we've given you, not to mention the sacrifices we've made for you," but the message the child receives may develop these feelings:

You don't love me, because you never hold me or cuddle me.

You yell at me all the time, then tell me you love me.

I get a hundred criticisms for every word of approval, so I must be no good. I am not loved.

Mother's actions may belie her words; her tone of voice may be in total disagreement with what she says. The child of such a parent may grow up to be a non-toucher, afraid of giving or receiving love, suspicious of people's motives, cold and aloof; or, depending upon numerous factors, he may become effusive and gushy, over compliant, sending out messages of insincerity, while feeling inward, "Love me, accept me, tell me I'm all right; touch me, affirm me, make up for all the loving and touching I failed to receive as a child."

Cultures and religions of all varieties have sought a common goal: the Nirvana of the Buddhists, the Satori of Zen, the Samadhi of the Hindus, the "peace that passes understanding" of the Christians. Could this longing for infinite peace and serenity be, not simply the reaction to life's stress, but an echo of the peace once experienced before birth? Or is it rather the haunting pre-conception memory of at-oneness experienced in a prebirth experience, when we were one with the Father?

No one can say with finality. All that is certain is that we are here, that we were damaged to some degree, that we are all different, and that we must learn to live together, to communicate more effectively, to love more deeply, or we shall all perish together.

You have no idea what a poor opinion I have of myself—and how little I deserve it.

— \N. S. Gilbert

SELF-REJECTION

It is not only parental "put-downs," sibling rivalry, or abuse and ridicule from authority figures that leave their mark. There are a thousand subtle forces impinging upon the delicate and sensitive fabric of the small child's emotional structure.

"DoN'T Touch Yourself Down There"

A young man whom I had known most of his life came to discuss with me a major crisis facing him. His wife wanted a divorce, and he was devastated.

They had been married only a few years, and he was very much in love with her.

One major complaint his wife had voiced was that he was virtually sexually impotent. There were other factors, but this one loomed largely. He wanted to know whether his impotence was physical or entirely psychological. I told him that in one his age, the problem was nearly always psychological.

He did feel vaguely reticent about sex, he told me, as though there was "something wrong, or bad or dirty" about it. I told him that in many instances, the mother is disturbed when a child touches the genital area. A typical reaction is for the mother to snatch the hand away, or slap it, and say, *"Stop that! That's dirty! Don't touch yourself down there."*
He gasped in surprise. *"I've seen my mother do that many times with my little sister, and she must have done it with me!"*
"Then," I said, "the child is conditioned to feel that there is something wrong with the genitals. It isn't a thought, or a conviction, just a vague, persistent feeling. Some people are able to overcome it, while others are seriously affected by it."
I asked him how he had felt about masturbation as a boy.
"Terrible," he said. *"That was something awful. I don't know precisely how or when or where I got the message, but I sensed that masturbation was forbidden, wrong, a sin against God."*
"Do you still feel that way?"
"Yes, I think I do. There's something vaguely bad about it. It is wrong, isn't it?"

I explained that most enlightened medical men, ministers, psychiatrists, and psychologists agree that there is absolutely nothing wrong with masturbation. It is, as Charlie Shedd expresses it in his excellent book The Stork Is Dead, "God's gift to the young"^ and, one might add, to the unmarried. He looked surprised at this totally new piece of information.

For many centuries children were savagely punished when suspected of what was termed "the solitary vice of self-abuse." The origin of this taboo is lost in antiquity, but it is known to be thousands of years old. The Egyptian Book of the Dead (1550 to 950 BC) refers to masturbation in negative terms.

Religious and medical authorities cooperated in trying to stamp out masturbation. Some medical men, until the early part of this century, though it was the cause of mental illness. No one knows how many women have found themselves sexually frigid, or partly so, as the result of misinformation of this sort, together with anxious cautioning calculated to prevent an unwanted pregnancy.

After repeated warnings not to "touch yourself down there" (much of it before the age of conscious memory), coupled with anxiety transmitted by parents about "getting into trouble," many women feel great anxiety and confusion about sex. A few minutes at the altar cannot erase mental and emotional conditioning that may begin in infancy and continue for years.

And much of the conditioning is not verbal. Where sex is seldom if ever mentioned in the home, children frequently grow up with a vague feeling that some monumental secret is being kept from them. If they seek to fathom the mystery on their own, they are often punished or made to feel guilty.

We can like ourselves better and relate better to people when we understand ourselves and the factors that made us the way we are. When we see the manifold ways in which personalities can be warped and damaged, it makes it easier to view ourselves and others with amused, friendly tolerance.

There Is No One to Blame

A kind word needs to be said about parents at this point. There is little organized effort to teach parents how to raise children. It is possible to get credit for a course in archery in numerous colleges and universities. One New York state college has offered a course in handicapping; that is, how to study racing forms and come to some conclusion as to which horse is most likely to win a given race. One may learn about rice tonnage in Indochina, the ocean currents adjacent to the Cape of Good Hope, fourth-century-B.C. Chinese art, the names of assorted kings, and a hundred wars. But relatively few courses are offered in either high school or college to prepare one for marriage and childrearing, two of the most complex tasks ever to face a human being.

Falling in love has little or nothing to do with working out a good marriage relationship, and conceiving a child bears little or no relationship to the arduous eighteen-year task of rearing a child. Yet in our present culture, it is assumed that falling in love is the main thing—which it isn't—and that childrearing will take care of itself—which it seldom does.

Neurotic Perfectionism It is not only verbal abuse, or neglect, that traumatizes children. They can be damaged by over-mothering, perfectionism, and unrealistic praise.

We cannot like ourselves, nor love ourselves properly, nor relate creatively to others, unless we understand what it is that motivates human beings.

Basically, the driving force is the need for:

- o Acceptance Approval Affection/Love
- o To be accepted means to be welcomed into the family, the tribe, the clan, the social group.

The opposite of this is *rejection*, one of the most painful of all experiences. Not to be accepted is to be an outcast, a reject. The feeling is 'T am not worthy; I am no good; there is something wrong with me." It is a very lonely feeling. Many children, for one reason or another, have felt this loneliness. Adults, who as children did not learn to relate easily to their peers, find this a devastating and depressing ongoing ordeal.

To experience approval is to win the affirmation of "significant others." To the child, this means approval by the family and close friends. Performance in school, indicated by grades, is one way children gain—or fail to gain—approval. The child usually seeks approval in terms of performance rather than for what he is as a person. It is easier to demonstrate worth with a report card or by performance in sports, in social activities, in music, in something we do, than to wait for people to recognize our worth as individuals.

AffectionlLove refers to the need to have people express warmth and affection for us, not because of what we do, but because they care about us as persons. Deep within every human, there is the need to be loved. Some have found early in life that "love hurts" and have shut the door on this tender emotion. Such people often become cynical. Others compensate by turning their energies into some endeavor where they can be admired, or at least noticed, if not loved. As a last resort, some become criminals in an effort to achieve notoriety in lieu of acceptance or love. In this way, they are at least "noticed."

From infancy on, the individual will go to almost any lengths to win approval, acceptance, and/or affection. Failing in this, some persons become depressed and apathetic; others act out their hurt aggressively, while still others become ill in an unconscious effort to gain sympathy or to be taken care of. The individual who talks interminably about his latest illness is, of course, seeking attention, first cousin to approval. One child in a family may win love and approval by being compliant and obedient. A sibling, finding the compliant slot already filled, may become aggressive and disobedient in an unconscious effort to win at least some attention.

'^Notice me!" is the universal cry that goes up from everyone, "if not because I am obedient, or nice, or lovable, then because I make good grades, or because I am good in sports, or something.'"

SUBSTITUTES FOR LOVE

Some standard compensations for the need to be important loved, and accepted, are these: the achieving of power, wealth, fame (or notoriety), degrees, titles, badges, citations, blue ribbons at the county fair, wall plaques, certificates—anything to certify that we are significant and worthwhile.

In order to achieve such distinctions, men and women have struggled, sacrificed, fought, schemed, lied, betrayed, and have even attempted acts of heroism and bravery. Others have become "saints"; if nothing else, one can be more godly or more humble, more something than others. The eternal silent cry goes up, "Notice me; tell me I am significant."

But when a child has been adequately loved— cuddled, touched, reassured—and nurtured by emotionally mature parents, there is no need for him to manipulate or overcompensate. He is not overly compliant nor overly aggressive. He doesn't have to prove anything in order to win love. You feel loved and secure.

I would not deprecate the human struggle to achieve and to attain some worthwhile goal. No one wishes to throw cold water on honest human endeavor. But the important thing in the struggle is to recognize the motivation. We must be honest with ourselves. Self-delusion is terribly devastating and damaging to the personality.

"ROLE" IS NOT "IDENTITY"

If a mother whose children have left the nest can be totally honest with herself, she will not meddle in their lives. She has done her job, well or poorly, as the case may be, and she should cut the cord. She is no longer a "mommy," but ideally a friend of her "former children."

But if she lacks true self-acceptance and has confused the role of mother with her identity, then she will need to counsel them, visit them, correct them, and their children, in an effort to feel significant.

Meddling mothers usually are those who never had any other identity than that of wife and mother. When deprived of those roles, they tend to feel useless and abandoned and often wallow in self-pity.

Our grown son wrote to me one day: 'I've decided to promote you. You are no longer my Dad, but any friend.'" I felt a wave of deep satisfaction as I read that.

The businessman who has been of value to his firm—and therefore feels significant—will do well to plan ten years in advance for his retirement. The time will come when he will no longer be needed by his firm. As a retired man, he loses significance unless he has discovered more meaning to life than working for Amalgamated Tool and Die Company, which, after all, is not an identity.

The people I know who truly like themselves as persons, apart from their roles in life as a husband, wife, parent, or job-holder, are those who have learned to be honest with themselves and who, to some degree, understand themselves. They are able to relate well with others because they like themselves and do not project their own buried self-hate onto those around them. Those who have learned to love themselves properly tend to love others.

You ask the meaning of life? Why are we here? It's simple. We're here to discover the meaning of life.

—C. Gillette

HOW GUILT, EMBARRASSMENT, AND A SENSE OF INFERIORITY CREATE A WEAK SELF-IMAGE

Sigmund Freud pointed out that it is almost impossible to distinguish between the feeling of guilt and the feeling of inferiority. I would add that shame, guilt, inferiority, and failure are different manifestations of the feeling of "worthlessness." Guilt, real or false, is probably the most damaging of all emotions.

It is terribly devastating to create in a child needless feelings of guilt, shame, and inferiority

MOST NEUROSES ARE ROOTED IN THE PAST

Psychologist Carl Rogers emphasizes the supreme importance of self-acceptance and self-understanding. He maintains that it is virtually impossible for one to understand and accept himself until someone has accepted him for what he is.

CAN WE BEAR THE GUILT OF OTHERS?

A person can suffer throughout life for the mistakes of a parent. Sometimes a parent, feeling responsible for the way a child turns out, develops a sense of guilt over the failure of the child. Agnes shared in our therapy groups her sense of disappointment and guilt over the fact that her daughter, who had left home, had become a lesbian. She said, "I find it hard even to say the word 'homosexual.' When she comes home at infrequent intervals with her girlfriend, I can feel only anger and self-pity. Or maybe it's guilt because I feel I failed her somewhere, but I don't know where."

The group encouraged her to talk out her feelings. No advice was offered since advice in these groups is considered an insult. Agnes felt greatly relieved when she could share her mixture of emotions with the group.

After a few more sessions, during which she discussed her problem and received the love and support of the group, she reported that she had at last been able to visit her daughter and the girl with whom she lived. She said, "I was able to tell them, sincerely, that I loved them." There was a look of deep satisfaction in her face as she related this.

Without condoning her daughter's way of life, she was giving understanding and love. In the act of expressing love, she felt released from her burden of guilt and self-pity.

There is an admonition in the New Testament that reads, *"Confess your sins [hurts, faults, needs] to one another, and pray for one another, that you may be healed"* (James 5:16, Rsv).

Agnes had obeyed this injunction. In sharing her hurt with the group, she was healed of her anger and depression and the guilt that surrounded the entire subject. Since self-love grows out of openness and honesty, Agnes came to have a far better self-image.

SELF-LOVE IS NOT BLUSTER AND ARROGANCE

Sometimes arrogant people give the superficial impression of total self-acceptance. In actuality, they do not like themselves. Their weak self-image is concealed beneath an aggressive facade. They have learned how to fake it. Occasionally, people with low self-esteem tend to admire these arrogant pretenders because they seem so self-assured, so confident, so utterly without self-doubt; but underneath their cloak of pretense, they are usually insecure persons who have learned to cover up their sense of inadequacy and self-rejection with a fake bluster or superficial sophistication.

But it is not only the false guilt others dump on us. There is the real guilt for which we must take responsibility. Whenever we violate our integrity, anytime we do something contrary to our ethical or moral code or fail to do what we believe we are supposed to do, we set in motion the incredibly complex guilt syndrome. I term it a "syndrome" because it has many facets and manifestations.

The inner judicial system knows only two verdicts: guilty or innocent. It knows no gray areas. It is inexorable. And once it has announced its verdict, it proceeds to execute justice. If the inner judicial system finds us guilty, it offers two options: either we must confess and accept forgiveness, or we must be punished.

It is not God who is speaking, but that portion of us that is called by such names as Conscience, Judicial System, Super Ego, the Inner Self. This part of the self is not necessarily the voice of God, for conscience is largely the product of our parents, our particular environment and culture.

Once the conscience has pronounced us guilty and declared that we must either be forgiven—by God and by ourselves—or be punished, it accepts no rationalizations. This portion of the self cannot be deluded, wheedled, or bought off. It accepts no excuses.

If we seek to make things right—by making restitution, asking pardon from God and man, or whatever else may be required—the conscience is satisfied. If for some reason, we cannot get a feeling of being forgiven, or if we refuse to alter our guilty conduct, the verdict is pronounced: how must be punished. And what a relentless and inexorable part of the personality this is!

Depending on one's type of personality, the verdict may involve becoming trouble-prone or accident-prone, thus having an accident to "pay the price of our defect," or one may "choose" a physical or emotional symptom.

SELF-HATE

Simon Peter hated himself, and he dissolved into bitter tears of self-recrimination. Only a little while before, he had made staunch affirmations of loyalty, and then he heard himself assert for the third time that he had nothing to do with Jesus of Nazareth. He was "not one of them,"; but no sooner had he uttered the denial than he saw Jesus turn and look at him. What was in that look? Reproof? Rebuke? Disappointment? Hurt?

"Peter, I knew you would fail me! You're weak, Peter. You've demonstrated that over and over. Why did I ever choose such an undependable person as you for a disciple? All the others have fled, and you followed me here to the trial, but now you—my last hope—have failed me."

No, nothing like that was intended to be conveyed in that glance. We know this by the amazingly tender way Jesus dealt with Simon Peter after the Resurrection. There was no direct reference to his denial, only a request for a threefold affirmation of love, to counterbalance the threefold denial.

But Peter must have read into that glance all sorts of things. He would have projected his own self-contempt and self-hatred onto Jesus and imagined the sternest rebuke. At any rate, he "went out and wept bitterly" (Matthew 26:75). Those were tears of remorse and self-loathing for his weakness.

I love Simon Peter. He is so like one of us, like someone I've known in the past and forgotten just when or where. He's familiar. Yes, now I've got it! He's like—not one of us—he's like me! No wonder I felt I'd known him. And if Jesus could treat him with such exquisite tenderness afterward, it tells me how I am going to be received, despite ten thousand failures and blunders.

I feel so sorry for the religious legalists who battered me as a child with a thousand fearful threats. I do not know who warped them, but it has been going on a long time, this matter of making God a vengeful Being to be feared, rather than a loving heavenly Father, who is like Jesus in his tender love for the wayward.

Someone defined a fundamentalist as "a person who is inexpressibly saddened by the knowledge that somewhere, somehow, someone is having a good time!" Those were the people of my childhood.

An ancient Persian text contains this gem: "There is no saint without a past—no sinner without a future." That would make a very suitable epitaph for Simon Peter—or you, or me.

GUILT — INDECISION AND INCOMPATIBLE GOALS

Guilt, at its core, is trying to pursue incompatible goals. Thus, the inner self is split, wanting two conflicting things and unable to achieve this impossible goal.

The emotion known as guilt functions basically likes an alarm clock. When the alarm goes off, it has served its purpose, and the awakened person normally turns it off. The alarm is "good" in that it alerts one to the fact that it is time to get up. It feels "bad" in that it awakens one from a sound sleep.

In daily life, when we violate our principles, the warning signal called "guilt" alerts us. We can feel a vague, gnawing sense of remorse, or uneasiness, or anxiety. This disquiet will continue until we have rectified the error and receive forgiveness. Then the feeling should dissipate. Half an hour is long enough to feel guilty about anything, once the issue has been resolved through repentance. Hopefully, one will examine the matter to make sure that it is not repeated.

It is not an irate God who is condemning us and making us feel uneasy and remorseful. It is the inner judicial system, which is much stronger in some people than in others. John Bunyan found great difficulty in feeling forgiven for having rung the church bell as a boyish prank. Other people commit serious crimes with less compunction. Conscience could be a vengeful, inexorable, vindictive foe if one were reared in an authoritative and punitive environment. Or, it can be so weak that, like a defective alarm clock, it gives only a mild tinkle or none at all.

You like yourself better when you have done what you feel you should have done, whether it involves paying all of your income tax, taking out the garbage, or visiting a sick friend. Failure to "do right" always registers as guilt, and you lose self-worth. You like yourself less well; then it becomes difficult, if not impossible, to love yourself. How can you learn to like or love a self that consistently fails to do the right thing?

SIN ERODES SELF-ESTEEM

In the matter of sins of commission, if you find yourself, through weakness or intent, doing something out of harmony with your own moral code, somewhere within you court has convened; the inner judge has seated himself on the bench; witnesses (in the form of thoughts, promises, commitments, memories) are called, and the trial begins. The trial moves with astonishing rapidity, unlike those trials where opposing attorneys rise every few minutes to raise objections.

This judicial system (conscience) is set up by God, not because he is unloving or vindictive, but because he loves us and wants us to live without inner conflict. He is anxious for us to live in harmony with a matchless set of universal principles that he established for our happiness and well-being.

Jesus said, *"Now you know this truth; how happy you will be if you put it into practice" (John 13:17, TeV).*

He was making it clear that our happiness and well-being are inexorably linked up with obeying the universal principles he had been teaching. To expect God's blessings and guidance without seeking to follow his formula would be as futile as asking God to "make it a good cake, Lord/' after we had failed to follow the recipe, or invoking his help in getting a car started without turning on the ignition.

This is not a capricious universe. It operates on unalterable principles, as much so in the spiritual realm as in the realm of physics or biology.

The traffic judge who fines us for going through a red light is not being unreasonable or vindictive. He is trying to remind us to be more careful, for our own sake and that of others. In the same spirit, our inner judge is anxious to guard our individual safety and well-being and the safety and well-being of those around us.

The inner judge, or conscience, is not an enemy, but our friend. He is on our side, no matter how often we may fail. His ultimate goal is to help us avoid all actions or attitudes that prevent us from loving ourselves properly. Conscience is not God, but his agent. Thus your inner judicial system seeks your safety and wholeness and well-being, just as our legal system functions to preserve the well-being of our society.

Some judges tend to be lenient; some, more severe. There are people whose inner judicial systems are overly strict and punitive; others have too lenient and lackadaisical a conscience. A discerning friend, pastor, or counselor can help you discover whether your conscience is overly strict or underdeveloped.

One thing is very clear: you can never love yourself properly as long as you violate divine principles. Obey your inner voice, and you will respect yourself Ignore it, and you will despise yourself

HOW TO DETERMINE IF YOU LACK A PROPER SELF-ESTEEM

The main word in this chapter is excessive. For instance, everyone is capable of being irritated at times. Excessive irritability suggests some degree of neurosis, a malfunctioning of the personality.

Here is a checklist to enable you to discover whether, or to what degree, you lack self-love.

✓ **Are you considered overly sensitive by friends or family?**

Most normal people have their feelings hurt on occasion. Few persons are totally immune to rejection or insult. The acid test is: Are you more easily offended than most people? Does it require a long time for you to recover from hurt?

Are you argumentative?

Some people feel an overwhelming urge to argue. They have an excessive need to prove their point. The ancient truth still applies: "A man convinced against his will is of the same opinion still."

Individuals with a weak sense of identity, if they happen to have aggressive temperaments, can seldom resist the temptation to debate any and all issues. They get involved in futile arguments about politics, religion (two subjects always best avoided where a big difference of opinion exists), books, morals, movies, TV shows, childrearing, or whatever they have strong feelings about.

Whether it be in taste in manners, religion, literature, politics, art, or food, there is no point in arguing about a matter where one person's opinion may be quite as valid as that of another. An amiable discussion is quite another matter.

✓ Are you a critical person?

An excessively critical attitude is a dead give-away. It reveals an individual who has a very poor opinion of himself. The worst critic is usually the one who is unconsciously most critical of himself. He dislikes himself intensely, and when he gets fed up with his own self-hate, he projects the rest onto those about him in the form of criticism. While striving to gain a greater degree of self-esteem, it is wise to stifle the impulse to be critical. It is more than a bad habit, for its roots go deep into one's self-rejection, but it is a habit, and it can be broken. Form the habit of focusing on the positive. Others will like you better, and that will enable you to like yourself better.

Are you intolerant of others? Of their ideas?

People who are intolerant of other races, religions, ideas or concepts, are broadcasting loud and clear: "I am a hostile, self-rejecting individual."

Gabriel Montalban once said, "There are a thousand shades of gray." As there are many colors and shades in the spectrum, so there is room for a wide variety of temperaments. It might simplify things if everyone thought as I do, and agreed with me, and liked what I like. But we are all uniquely different, just as every snowflake that ever fell to earth has a different pattern. God seems to dislike exact duplicates, n. God seems to dislike exact duplicates.

Yet, most of us, at times, are puzzled, or even angered, those other people can feel and think so differently. It seems a bit strange to me that some people eat snails, that many business people in the Middle East sit around a good part of the day smoking hubble-bubble pipes, that Eskimos eat blubber, that millions of people flock daily to cocktail bars and talk trivia. New Year's Eve celebrations strike me as ridiculous, chiefly, because I dislike crowds.

Extreme left-wingers and rabid right-wingers appall me. Why can't they be well-balanced like I am, a staunch progressive, anxious to preserve the values of the past but willing to explore new methods and ideas? All extremists puzzle or frighten me.

Why can't men wear their hair like mine? And dress as I do? Why do young people affect that ridiculous, outlandish, sloppy attire?

But hold on a minute! Why shouldn't people eat snails or snakes for that matter? I am told that rattlesnake meat tastes very much like chicken. As for the hubble-bubble pipe smokers, if they find life more pleasant that way, who am I, a mere compulsive worker, to object to their lifestyle? Eskimos, I hear, need fat for metabolic purposes. The avid party-goers simply rate higher on social needs than I do. And why should it bother me that people want to whoop it up on New Year's Eve? Why can't I let them do their thing? As for the left- and right-wingers, I now recall having led a wildcat strike at a Detroit automobile plant in my youth—and got fired for my radicalism. I'd forgotten about that. The political extremists are exercising their constitutional rights. Why should that bother me, excessively?

And hairstyles and matters of dress? My distaste for styles and ideas divergent from mine tells me that I am really asking, "Why can't people be more like me?" That's a pretty egotistical stance, now that I come to think of it.

✓ Are you an excessively angry person?

Do you "blow up" easily? Anger is not evil. It is a God-instilled survival emotion. All human emotions are divine in origin, given to us for our protection. God wants us to survive.

What is evil is the misuse of anger. We have a right to our feelings. Children should never be punished for expressing their emotions. They should be guided as to when and where to express them.

When you are outraged, go to your room and express your rage. Talk it out. Shout and scream if you feel like it. Don't sound nice and pious. Be real! All emotions are valid.

Then write a letter. Tell the offender off! Make it strong. Don't mince words. Forget all about tact and reasonableness. But having written it, don't mail it, of course! Just let it lie there for a few days. Read it again later, and smile at the blind rage you felt. You will never forget the relief experienced by expressing your honest feelings.

The key is this: We have a right to our anger, but we do not have the right to dump our hostility on other people and crush them. We usually get most angry when we have been insulted or abused in some way. With us, it is usually a personal thing. The more passive person accepts criticism or abuse, feels that he cannot express his hurt, and turns it inward. His subsequent depression is the result of what is termed "inwardly directed hostility."

He has buried his anger. It doesn't go away; it is transmuted into depression or a physical symptom. The aggressive individual who has been offended tends to erupt and feels justified in attacking the object of his wrath. Others, neither very passive nor aggressive, may alternate between turning their anger inward occasionally and expressing it in some way.

✓ Are you forgiving?

Some years ago, I spent a few hours with a relative who was then around ninety. I had not seen him for many years and remembered him as an exceptionally hostile person. Now I saw that age had eroded his explosive nature somewhat. He appeared much calmer. Sometimes the approaching of the Angel of Death does instill in one a greater capacity for gentleness.

But as he reminisced, he showed some of his old spirits. Relating something that had happened sixty years before in a small town in Texas, he grew more and more tense, then hostile, and finally bitter. I could see that he still had traces of the old unforgiving spirit that had marked him when he was younger. Sixty years seems a long time to carry a grudge.

Those who do not love themselves have a weak self-image, and it is often very difficult for them to forgive. It is as though they would lose something precious were they to extend the olive branch. Lacking the "glue" of self-respect and proper self-love to hold the personality together, they use the adhesive of old hates and grudges. Though they are usually unaware of the process, it goes like this: 'T cannot forgive myself; thus, I cannot forgive anyone else."

The unforgiving person does irreparable harm to his personality. The human organism functions far better when there is a sense of "being at peace." When a grudge is held, there can be no serenity. The grudge creates stress, and continued stress is destructive of the organism. Excessive, continued stress paves the way for a host of physical symptoms: ulcers, heart attacks, asthma, neurodermatitis (a severe skin condition that seldom yields to medication), migraine headaches, colitis, rheumatoid arthritis, and many others.

This is not to say that repressed hostility alone causes such symptoms, but it is usually a component.

The message is clear: We cannot pray or worship effectively, nor meet the conditions for receiving God's blessings if we are spiritually and emotionally out of harmony, filled with stress and conflict created by impaired relationships. We cannot love ourselves properly when we are unforgiving. We are out of synchronization with God's beautiful cosmic harmony that seeks to bless and guide us.

✓ **Are you excessively jealous?**

The word excessive is used here, since everyone is, to some degree, capable of jealousy.^ Possessiveness and jealousy usually go together. They are often the product of childhood experiences or influences, rendering the individual very insecure.

Though everyone is capable of jealousy to some degree, it is only when it becomes excessive that it interferes seriously with relationships or one's peace of mind. Pathological jealousy and possessiveness place too much of a burden on a relationship. One husband, whose wife could not endure for him to be out of her sight except during working hours, finally said to her, 'T don't know the source of your problem, but your possessiveness is killing me, and I have no intention of putting up with it indefinitely. You must get some professional help, or I will want a divorce. This is not a threat but an honest feeling."

She came to me for counseling, and we quickly discovered that her jealousy related to her father, who had disappeared when she was a little girl. She had been fearful and insecure ever since. In time, her deep insecurity yielded to In-Depth Therapy.

If you find yourself inordinately jealous or possessive, you can be sure that you lack self-love. One with such deep insecurities finds it very difficult to develop proper self-esteem. Intensive therapy is usually indicated, not simplistic advice or positive thinking.

✓ **Are you a poor listener?**

I once had a friend who had a remarkable store of jokes, which he told well. He was a splendid public speaker and used his stories and jokes to excellent advantage. But he was never known to laugh, or even smile, at jokes told by anyone else. When he was the center of attention, his eyes sparkled. When the conversation veered away from him, his eyes glazed over. He was a good speaker, but a poor listener.

Such a person is so preoccupied with his own feelings and his own self-importance that he simply cannot bring himself to listen to anyone else. He is, in short, a self-centered, not a self-loving person. One who is at peace with himself can forget himself part of the time. If you accept yourself, like yourself, believe in yourself, you can endure having the conversation, include others, and listen with interest.

Someone reported, "I used to respond to most things people said with 'Baloney,' and I had very few friends. Then I changed, and began to say 'Marvelous,' and now I'm invited everywhere." His semifacetious comment contains more than a grain of truth.

The appreciative listener, though he may have to "fake" it until it becomes a habit, is exhibiting an inferior-talent trait. In time, he will come to like himself better because listening can be an act of love; and we always like ourselves better when we act in love.

✓ **Are you excessively materialistic? Do you have a poverty complex?**

There is always a perfectly valid explanation for any neurosis.*^ When I discover the childhood source of a person's neurosis, I invariably find myself feeling understanding, concern, and compassion. But the world at large is not going to take the time to try to understand the origin of our neurotic behavior patterns.

If you have a poverty complex, it will seem the most rational thing in the world to you. I have a friend who has his garage, two rooms of his home, the patio, the shed, and part of the yard, piled high with what I would call junk. To him, it has enormous value: 'T might need that someday," he tells his patient but a frustrated wife.

He has accumulated this amazing collection of mechanical and electrical junk through the years. He can justify each piece, most of which rusts or rots long before he has an opportunity to catalog it, much less use it.

He experienced poverty and emotional deprivation in childhood, though not more than millions of other children. In addition, there was a mentally unstable mother and an absentee father. The combination caused his insecurity to take the form of a pack-rat complex.

I have a mild poverty complex and am a collector. I collect ancient artifacts, such as Roman glassware, amphora from the Aegean Sea, pottery from two to four thousand years old, and the like. I would like to believe that this is rooted solely in a love of beauty and ancient civilizations, but I am aware that this is only partly true. It originates in mild insecurity. Like all complexes, this originated in childhood. I recall hearing my mother say in a manner that irritated me even at age four: "No, we can't afford that." For some reason, I translated that to mean "We're poor," and be A true miser, or a person with a full-blown poverty complex, saves ridiculous things for absurd reasons, and the degree of the hangup is the measure of the insecurity lurking in that person's personality. Insecurity is based on fear, and one with a great deal of fear usually has comparatively little self-love.

One who truly loves himself can have wealth without pride, or poverty without humiliation. He is fundamentally "nonattached." He takes neither life nor himself too seriously. His center is in himself rather than in persons or things. He can rejoice in beauty and possessions, or lose them without loss of serenity. In loving God, his neighbor, and himself, his basic needs are met, because all things of value flow out of that triangular love affair with God, others, and self.

✓ **Are you greatly impressed by titles, degrees, honors, badges**?

There is nothing fundamentally wrong with titles, degrees, and honors. They become deterrents to emotional and spiritual growth only when one values them excessively.

If without too much struggle or at too great a sacrifice, one is able to win some honors or certificates or blue ribbons, or if society insists on bestowing them, fine. But the tense preoccupation with status symbols is something else. One who fully accepts himself and loves himself properly can be happy without certification by others, but if honors are awarded, he can accept them graciously and value them for what they are: mild expressions of appreciation or evidence of success in pursuit of some significant goal. They would mean something to him, but he would not overvalue them.

I, who was very grateful for having an honorary degree awarded me many years ago, like to think what Jesus might have said had some prestigious institution offered him such an honor. My private conviction is that he would undoubtedly have smiled, waved his arm toward that mixed rabble following him, and said something like, *"These are my prizes, my awards. I have no greater need than that they love me, obey me, and follow me."*

At the present state of our spiritual development, most of us probably need our badges, titles, degrees, and certificates of merit. I do not deprecate them. I simply suggest that they are viewed as props for sagging egos, to keep us going until we can gain a greater degree of self-love.

✓ **Are you a poor loser?**

Phillip is a highly successful surgeon. He is personable, cheerful, nice-looking, and appears to be a well-integrated personality. One glaring symptom that turned up in his counseling sessions was the fact that he is one of the world's worst losers.

In fact, he never loses. If necessary, he cheats in order to win the game. Worse still, even playing games with his own children—checkers, croquet, or touch football—he consistently cheats, or will insist on playing "just one more game" until he can win.

Here is blatant evidence of a weak ego. Although he has achieved significantly as an adult, his childhood was marked by so much rejection that he feels not quite acceptable either to himself or to others. "Losing" represents a loss of self-esteem to him.

People who easily lose their tempers in playing games—or in an argument, for that matter—reveal something important about themselves: They do not like themselves. Aggressive self-haters will fight, argue, contend, or even cheat to win; more passive self-haters tend more often to go into depression, or at least become moody, a manifestation of mild depression.

✓ Do you find it hard to accept compliments?

According to a study conducted at Colorado State University, two out of three people feel uncomfortable when paid a compliment. Half of the 245 subjects surveyed felt obligated to return the compliments or reciprocate in some fashion. Thirty percent felt they would appear conceited if they failed to neutralize the compliments gracefully, and twenty percent suspected that ulterior motives lay behind the praise. "Compliments often give rise to uneasiness, defensiveness, and cynicism," according to Professor Ronny Turner, who conducted the survey. There was a tendency, upon receiving a verbal compliment, to say, *"Oh, you say such nice things"; 'T had lots of help"; 'It was really nothing"; 'It would have been better if. . ."; "I was lucky";* or wait for the compliments to be followed by criticism. Other typical responses from the majority were, *'T can't take all the credit"; "Anyone could have done it"; "This old thing? I've had it for years."*

There is a basic psychological law to this effect: We tend to act in harmony with our self-image. If our self-image (self-respect, self-love, self-worth) is weak, a compliment may be out of harmony with the way we perceive ourselves, in which case we tend to reject it.

What can one say, then, that does not seem conceited, nor yet self-abasing? Self-accepting people respond with neither "Oh, I thought my performance was awful!" or "Yes, I agree I was pretty wonderful." Instead, a simple "Thank you" suffices. By practicing that, one can overcome any mild embarrassment when praise is offered.

TEST TO DETERMINE THE DEGREE OF YOUR SELF-ACCEPTANCE

Answer True or False to the following questions the way you genuinely feel:

1)   I received from my parents about all the love I needed.

2)   I am no more self-conscious than the average person.

3)   I seldom feel terribly critical of people.

4)   I have about as many friends as I would like.

5)   It doesn't bother me much when people I know do some do something really stupid.

6)   I think I have gotten about as much as I deserve from life.

7)   I have not been bothered by many physical or emotional symptoms.

8)   I tend to trust most people without too much difficulty.

9)   Politicians are about as honest as the average person.

10) I am probably no more sensitive than most people.

11) It seldom occurs to me. People might be laughing at me.

12) Most people won't let you down in a pinch.

Count the number of Trues checked.

1. If you checked all twelve Trues, you have a very remarkable sense of self-acceptance.

2. Ten indicates a high degree of self-acceptance.

3. Eight is indicative of a very good degree of self-acceptance.

4. Six is average.

5. Anything below six suggests a rather weak self-image.

*What a man thinks of himself...
determines his fate.*

— Henry David Thoreau

WHAT SELF-LOVE IS NOT

Although the terms self-love, self-acceptance, self-esteem, and self-approval are not precisely synonymous, there is a sense in which we can use them interchangeably. For our purposes in this chapter, we can refer to self-accepting people as those who love themselves.

THE SELF-ACCEPTING PERSON IS NOT DRIVEN BY NEUROTIC AMBITION.

A psychiatric dictionary defines ambition as "a defense against shame." It is a shame of being or feeling inferior to others. This does not disparage the legitimate desire to attain some worthwhile goal.

An excessive drive to excel, to win over others, to stand out, to be superior, to be the richest, the most powerful, to have the most of something, springs not from proper self-love, but often from a deep sense of inferiority.

Alfred Adler, one of Freud's early disciples, came to feel that the basic human urge was not the sex drive, as Freud had postulated, but the drive to excel, to overcome one's feelings of weakness and helplessness; in short, to compensate for feelings of inferiority.

Competitiveness has its place, particularly in games and sports, but emotionally mature people learn to compete only with their previous best, not with others. (Someone has pointed out that the world's best swordsman has nothing to fear from the world's second-best swordsman, but he had better flee in haste from an angry farmer with a pitchfork.) One should compete, if at all, in his own field, and with the awareness that others may be more greatly endowed.

Personally, I don't want to compete with anyone, in any realm. If I were to compete with someone, I might discover that his natural endowments are less than mine, and my goal would, therefore, be too low; or his abilities may far outstrip mine, and I could become discouraged.

True self-esteem can give one a quiet determination to surpass his previous performance. That might involve anything from trying to win two blue ribbons instead of the one received last year or to decide to live life more fully than heretofore.

<u>SELF-ACCEPTING PEOPLE DO NOT EXPECT OTHERS TO MAKE THEM HAPPY OR MEET ALL THEIR NEEDS.</u>

A woman who consulted me about a marriage problem seemed to be making unreasonable demands of her husband. Some of her expectations were reasonable, but the rest, I felt, were leftover needs from childhood. I said, "I expect your husband is capable of meeting most of your valid needs, but many of your expectations seem to be childhood needs your parents failed to meet. If you continue demanding that your husband meet both your childhood and adult needs, you will drive him right out of the nest."

"But he ought to meet my needs," she said. "I have a right to expect it! What is marriage for? He's selfish not to meet these needs. If he really loved me. ..." She went on for a long time, in a strained, petulant, demanding voice. I was saddened that her parents had not given her the love she required, for it had left her an unfulfilled, complaining woman, making unrealistic demands.

When I explained that no one person could meet all of our needs, she looked at me blankly. "But that shouldn't be! It isn't right. Why does anyone get married then?" Her marriage ended in divorce, and she is still fruitlessly searching for a man who will meet all of her needs.

<u>ONE WHO HAS SELF-ESTEEM IS NOT OVER COMPLIANT.</u>

The excessively over compliant individual has the unconscious goal of winning love and approval from everyone. Such a person finds it almost impossible to say no. This tendency usually originates early in childhood, as the result of a need to win parental love when the child has some reason to doubt that love.

How People Become, Overcompliant Kathy was reliving a buried memory from her earliest childhood during an In-Depth counseling session. She experienced herself seated on the floor, playing while her mother and a neighbor were talking.

She heard her mother say, "I didn't want a fourth child. This kid has been crying ever since she was born. I really didn't need another child.

" Kathy, talking not about her mother but to her, screamed, "Mommy, mommy, don't say that! Don't say that! I'll be good; I'll do anything, anything if you won't ever say that again!" Kathy wept for half an hour over the agonizing realization that she was not wanted. As a child, she never cried again and became a company totally, not only with her mother but with everyone else. She said later, "I know now, for the first time, why I have never been able to say no to anyone. In reliving that experience, I felt myself making a lifetime vow to give in and do whatever mommy or anyone else wanted if only they would love me." With this insight, Kathy also discovered why she had been sexually permissive. People who cannot say no are usually overcommitted, because of their great need to accede to every request. They often feel rushed and hectic and complain of being terribly busy. Their weak sense of identity is excessively dependent upon feeling needed.

Kathy embarked on a course of learning to say no when it was appropriate. I told her that at first, it would be very difficult and that she might find it easier initially to reply, "Yes, I'd be glad to [giving herself time to think], but I won't be able to fit it into my schedule." This avoided the use of the self-forbidden "no," and allowed her the right to refuse when it seemed appropriate.

A delightful friend of mine, a minister, said ruefully, "I have a character by consensus. I invariably have to find out what other people think or feel, and then I always agree with them. I hate myself for it!" Undoubtedly, if he were to search in the primal feelings not accessible to the conscious mind, he would find, as Kathy did, that he had made a similar vow to be super compliant.

Many people of outstanding ability, as the result of childhood conditioning, have been rendered over-compliant. Charles Darwin was so fearful of his father's disapproval that he delayed twenty-six years before publishing his world-shaking theory of organic evolution.

<u>ONE WITH SELF-ESTEEM IS NOT EASILY DEFEATED. HISTORY RECORDS THE CASE OF</u>

a shiftless, rolling stone of a husband married to an illegitimate girl from the Virginia mountains. He tried five or six farms and kept moving on, a man afflicted, we'd say today, with a character neurosis, who thought that by picking a new place, like a movie actress who keeps picking a new husband, he would somehow change the plot. He didn't, of course. They plodded into Indiana and did a little better. In time, they had a barn, and a few animals, a little corral, a rail fence, and they planted corn and flax and

Beans. But then the neighbors came down with the 'milk sickness,' picked up from cows that chewed on snakeroot. Our farmer's wife died.

 So the vagabond father and soon moved on to a new state and new ground, the son passing from an almost animal boyhood into bleak manhood; yet out of that frail woman and her listless husband and the poorest ground, there came something strange and wholly admirable: the slow-moving son who seized a Republic and held it through its first cataclysm—Abraham Lincoln.^

And of course, everyone is familiar with the innumerable setbacks he suffered before becoming president —a business failure that saddled him with the debts of a dishonest partner; failure after failure as he sought public office; but some subtle combination of will, determination, and innate, homespun wisdom and intelligence, and a character rooted and grounded in simple faith in God, provided him with sufficient self-esteem and inner strength to triumph over every obstacle.

<u>WINNING WITHOUT LOVE</u>

How can we account for these bruised and battered children of misfortune and hardship who, in defiance of all laws of probability, succeed in reaching their goals? Bob is a delightful, humorous young man in his early thirties whom I have come to know and admire. His father is a half-breed Crow, his mother, a mixed-race Cherokee. They met on the reservation. The grandparents with eleven children had been moved from an Indian reservation to the West Coast in a boxcar. Two children died of dysentery on the way.

Bob grew up on the West Coast among lumber people. "My nickname was 'Worthless.' I'd do anything, no matter how demeaning just to get a few positive strokes," he said. When he was nine, he began felling timber with a chain saw. His back was broken twice; his left leg shattered several times, his right leg once, and both arms and eighteen ribs were smashed in logging accidents.

A few months before he was eleven, because he refused to work for an older brother without being paid, his father ordered him out of the house. He went to work for a neighboring farmer for a dollar a day, milking sixteen cows night and morning, together with other chores. He worked there two years, then gravitated to Alaska, where he worked on a fishing boat. Entirely on his own, he worked his way through high school.

"I was befriended by the part-time pastor of a local church. He was a very warm, loving, accepting kind of person, and through him, I was led to Christ. He encouraged me to continue my education. Eventually, I finished college, then went on to seminary." Bob now pastors a growing Baptist church in the Northwest. He says, "Of all the tragedies in my life, the one that weighs the heaviest is the death of my mother-in-law several years ago. My wife came from a very warm, affirming home, and I had developed a close relationship with her parents. It was very rewarding. They became my surrogate parents, of course, taking the place of the ones who utterly rejected me."

Bob still has areas of insecurity, like most people, but he has managed to surmount a host of obstacles. From some inner reservoir, he drew strength to survive, and from a loving, concerned minister and his wife's parents, he received the love and affirmation that enabled him to continue against all the odds.

The general rule is that we learn to love by having been loved in childhood. The deprivation of this love, in most instances, is terribly damaging to the personality. For reasons not clearly understood as yet, there are people who have a high-survival factor, who manage to survive, achieve significantly, and learn to love, despite a wretched start in life. These are self-accepting people who, in accepting themselves as okay, come to believe that they can not only survive, but also learn to give and receive love.

The Bible portrays its heroes with their weaknesses as well as their strengths. It makes no effort to gloss over their defects. Particularly in his youth, David was hot-tempered and impetuous.

He was easily insulted and quick to take offense, but he was equally ready to apologize and make amends. We do ourselves and others a great disservice when we imply—or teach—that Christians will never be angry. Of course, we will! Everyone is capable of anger to some degree. We can all be irritated or frustrated. It is simply a part of our humanity. The Bible does not teach that we will not have these emotions; it simply urges us to control them. If we fail, as we often will, we are to make amends.

GENIUS AND SELF-ACCEPTANCE

A biographer describes Beethoven as so touchy and overly sensitive that he bordered on paranoia. His closest friends were on occasion liable to find themselves excluded because of some imagined slight. He became increasingly morose and suspicious.

He lacked the capacity for a sustained relationship with people, and particularly with a woman, though he desired it very much. His enormous aggression was sublimated in his music, or he might have succumbed to some degree of paranoid schizophrenia.

Beethoven was quite well aware of his musical genius, and he did not doubt for an instant that he would rank as one of the world's greatest composers, but there is little evidence that he accepted or liked himself as a person.

It seems unfortunate that the gift of genius so often predisposes one toward emotional lopsidedness. One eminent psychologist has suggested that a certain excessiveness is essential to significant achievement; that those who are "too well balanced" emotionally seem to be on dead center. A significant achievement is often purchased at the price of emotional balance. Those whose goal is contentment and inner serenity are willing to forego the pleasure of greater achievement. Though this seems to be the general rule, it cannot be construed as a psychological law.

The overly sensitive individual is often hypercritical. He tends to project his own self-rejection onto others in the form of either criticism, sarcasm, or some other thinly veiled form of hostility. A woman who had made amazing spiritual growth in a Yokefellow group wrote to me as follows:

I hadn't been getting along well with people. They irritated and angered me and made me resentful, yet from somewhere inside of me, I felt great loneliness that would rise up and consume me. I did not know what to do at these times except to strike out at those around me in the hope that they would notice me, even though I knew I was most obnoxious.

When I entered my Yokefellow group over two years ago, I was driven by a fear that overwhelmed me—a fear that someday I might kill another person. I hated everyone around me, and most of all, myself, for the person I had become. I fluctuated between suicidal depression and violence aimed at others.

The Yokefellow group first showed me that there was a way to handle the violence within me, by facing each resentment as it came, dealing with it, and releasing it. I learned that if I hoarded these resentments, sooner or later, there would be an explosion over which I had no control—something like an atom bomb. What a relief now that I have learned to handle my anger!

I am particularly grateful to Yokefellows, and the weekly evaluation slips for putting into words the feelings I have always known I had, but couldn't verbalize. I had knowledge of my feelings before joining the group, but not the insight to go along with the emotions. I was living on pure emotion, and was headed for my third breakdown, and knew I must try, with God's help to put a stopper in the basin before I went down the drain for the last time.

<u>SELF-ACCEPTING PEOPLE LEARN TO HANDLE THEIR ANGER APPROPRIATELY.</u>

Many people firmly believe that all anger is evil. This attitude usually originates in false religious teaching that assumes that to be "truly Christian," one must avoid displaying anger at all costs. However, I have found some persons who, though not reared in a religious environment, learned from parents or other authority figures that all anger is forbidden.

Albert, a young man in his late twenties, discussed with me the problem of his uncontrollable anger. In the army, he had, at various times, been demoted, censured, and almost court-martialed for his violent displays of anger toward superior officers. I said, "Albert, you are assuming that anger is the problem, and I think it is only the symptom. The problem is probably fear, so deeply buried that you are unaware of it. It manifests itself as anger. Let's search for ancient fear."

"No," he said, "I know myself; it's anger. I've always had trouble with it, even as a child. Won't you pray with me that it will go away?" I replied that I would pray for a solution for whatever it was that troubled him.

Albert got no relief. A few years later, having married, he came to see me about a very disabling phobia that was causing him considerable grief. He had agoraphobia, "fear of open places." He could travel only in a very restricted area and could venture outside the limits of his self-imposed prison only if he were accompanied by his wife or some trusted friend.

I said, "Albert, we are dealing now with something that bears a relationship to your anger. Much anger originates in buried fear, and your fear that has now become a phobia with deeply buried origins can be uncovered only with intensive therapy. We have delayed too long already. Let's get to work on the buried roots of your fear. Often there is buried guilt, real or false, at the bottom. Shall we start to work?"

"No," he replied, "I don't want all this psychological stuff; I just want the simple gospel. It must be removed by prayer. Prayer can remove mountains. I am a firm believer in the Word." I said, "My friend, we will be praying only about the symptom of something much deeper, believe me." He refused to consider the possibility.

That was years ago. I saw him recently, now a man of sixty who looked seventy, shuffling along the street with a fixed, false smile that never left his face. I learned that his wife had divorced him, rather than live with his proliferation of phobias. "But," he said, with his plastic, fixed smile, "I couldn't be happier. The Lord is with me. Things are really wonderful, beautiful." He shuffled on, within the limits of his greatly constricted prison, which now includes only a few blocks, beyond which he dare not venture. Because of his refusal to search for the roots of his anger and guilt, he is forever imprisoned by his fears.

.

<u>NO ONE CAN MAKE YOU HAPPY</u>

No one can make us happy. Others may contribute to our happiness, but it is childish and unrealistic to expect someone else to make us happy. Sigmund Freud wrote, "What is called happiness in its narrowest sense comes from the satisfaction—most often instantaneous —of pent-up needs which have reached great intensity, and by its very nature can only be a transitory experience.

No one is happy all the time. We must settle for that first cousin of happiness, contentment; the wise are "content with contentment," studded with occasional peaks of happiness.

BENEFITS OF SELF-LOVE

People who love themselves properly tend to have fewer illnesses, live longer, are happier, less accident-prone, and more successful, have better families and fewer troubles, and make better decisions.

That is a very broad, all-inclusive generalization. It reads at first glance like a testimonial for patent medicine. Let's see whether there is any factual evidence to support it.

First, let it be said that there appear to be some exceptions to all rules, including this one. Bad things happen to good people, as Job discovered. Jesus died on a cross; the apostle Paul suffered innumerable hardships and indignities, including imprisonment, shipwreck, and persecution.

However, mounting scientific evidence is being amassed at a prodigious rate indicating that self-hate can play a part in everything from head colds and accident-proneness to headaches, intestinal problems, and cancer.

Let's take a look at some of the concrete scientific evidence linking disturbed emotions and illness.

Emotions and Dis-Ease Disease originally meant, not an illness, but lack of ease: dis-ease. In other words, not to be at ease within oneself promotes disease. With the discovery that illness is caused by germs, it was assumed that all one had to do in order to remain well was to avoid germs. This, however, did not explain why a person becomes ill at one time and not another; why, in the midst of a flu epidemic, one could remain well, yet fall victim to the flu six months or five years later when no one else around him suffered. Why, during a cold epidemic, do some people remain seemingly immune?

Recent studies reveal that the life expectancy of American men increased by only three years between 1900 to 2000, despite all of the advances in surgery, antibiotics, anesthesia, and the elimination of smallpox and yellow fever. Women's life expectancy increased by seven years during the same period. There appears to be some unknown factor at work, increasing longevity for women faster than for men.

Groups of researchers have been studying the relationship between emotions and illness and longevity since the late 1930s. Dr. Harold G. Wolff, a neurologist at the Cornell University Medical College and New York Hospital, was one of the pioneers in the study of psychosomatic medicine. He and his associates discovered evidence that certain life events tend to trigger many kinds of illnesses, including colds, skin disease, and tuberculosis.

Another group of researchers working along the same lines explored the relationship between emotions and illness among 5,000 patients. Life-changing events, even minor ones, such as the visit of a mother-in-law and stress of almost any kind, predisposed the patients to many different forms of illness.

They found that illness tended to follow a cluster of events that required some type of life-adjustment. The changes in life-pattern tended to occur in a two-week period before the onset of some illnesses, which included tuberculosis, heart disease, skin disease, hernia, and kindred ailments. Life-changing events listed were such

Ordinary occurrences as trouble with in-laws, a son or daughter leaving home, financial difficulties, loss of a job, changing to a different type of work, and change of residence or change in school. Even vacation, retirement, and sometimes significant personal achievement seemed related to illness. Some people are unable to accept the outstanding good news. It is out of harmony with their self-image and hence causes emotional stress, the forerunner of illness in many instances.

Ten different life-changes were assigned a value, the one rated at 100 being the death of a spouse, with these following: divorce, marital separation, jail term, death of a close family member, personal injury, marriage, being fired, marital reconciliation, retirement.

One group of researchers worked with 2,500 officers and enlisted men aboard three US Navy cruisers.

They gathered life-change data for six months preceding embarkation, and health change data for a six-month period starting with the beginning of the cruise. Results showed that the men in the high-risk group (those having the greatest number of life changes) suffered nearly ninety percent more illnesses than the low-risk group.

STRESS, EMOTIONS, AND SELF-ESTEEM

On the basis of weighty evidence, scientists now believe that beyond all possibility of doubt, there is a close relationship between stress —from whatever source—and illness.

Medical men at the famous Oschner Clinic of New Orleans believe that seventy-six percent of the people who visit the clinic are suffering from psychosomatic illnesses, rather than diseases of physical origin.

The disturbance is real, of course, but it has an emotional component. The school system of one of the largest cities in California estimated that seventy-five percent of ailments reported by children are emotionally induced.

Let's take a look at accidents. A considerable body of evidence indicates that, as Carl Jung postulated, the less well-integrated a person is, the more adverse circumstances he seems to attract to himself. During my forty-six years of counseling, I have had ample opportunity to observe thousands of people and their reactions to life. I recall many persons who seemed to attract accidents, illness, and disaster as a magnet attracts iron filings. These were invariably either insecure, fearful, apprehensive individuals, who, though often outwardly cheerful, inwardly were self-rejecting persons, or individuals experiencing severe inner conflicts. Some attracted frequent illnesses, others were given to frequent hospital stays, while many were involved in repetitious accidents.

As Jung has pointed out, the better integrated an individual is; that is, the more self-esteem he possesses, the more "good things" he attracts to himself. Jung did not explain how it worked; he simply made the observation.

CONFLICT, SELF-HATE, AND FAILURE

I recall a young minister whom I had occasion to know quite well over a period of fifteen years. He had ability and drive, despite a fairly limited educational background. During the period I knew him, he was hospitalized a number of times with severe and inexplicable infections of a very virulent type—always the same kind. These hospitalizations invariably followed periods of severe stress in his church.

He suffered a number of accidents, for which he did not seem to be directly responsible. Finally, I noticed a gradual change. He became rather manic—excited, tense, and very "high." His friends interpreted it as a strong dose of enthusiasm, for he was embarking on a large expansion program. I learned later that about this time, he began to drink excessively.

Eventually, he ended up with a series of hospitalizations, followed by a stay in a mental hospital. Upon release, there was more heavy drinking. He finally disintegrated completely. He sought no form of counseling from any source and avoided me during his period of great stress. He ultimately disappeared from the scene after writing a number of bad checks. His was a complete emotional, spiritual, physical, and moral disintegration, which was tragic to watch.

It would be easy to judge him as simply a moral failure. My conviction is that his deep-seated sense of inferiority made it difficult for him to accept himself as a person of worth. He attempted to compensate for his inferiority complex by attaining some significant goals. When that effort failed, and he tried to deaden his disappointment with alcohol, he lost all hope. It is possible, too, that some metabolic dysfunction was at work, either causing or caused by his various personal disasters.

Joseph was a slave in Egypt, though a very valued and trusted one. When his employer's wife sought to seduce him, he might have rationalized it this way: "If I do not give in to her demands, she will get me into trouble. Survival is important. I don't want this scheming woman to become my enemy." And besides, there was his own ever-present sex drive to underscore such a rationalization.

You know the story. He rejected her advances. Then as now, "hell hath no fury as a woman scorned." She raised a cry, claiming that he had tried to attack her. Joseph ended up in jail (Genesis 39).

A prison is a lonely place, and prison fare has never been very good. In ancient Egypt, it must have been rotten. We are not told how long Joseph languished in his cell, but surely it was an unpleasant reminder that the path of virtue could be rough.

Everyone likes a happy ending. But let's leave him in prison for the time being. Prison life is hard, but Joseph knows one thing: he is innocent and can sleep with a clear conscience! He has his self-respect. He can love himself properly. He has done nothing wrong. If he rots in prison, as millions have done throughout history, he can live with himself through the cold nights and the lonely days. Whether the story ends happily or otherwise is not the point, because virtue does not always get one out of prison, or bring wealth and fame. The honest, decent, moral person in some instances will suffer injustice, with only the comforting assurance that he does not deserve it. In his despair, he can live with himself and love himself for doing right. It's hard to do the will of God, but it's hell if you don't.

PATIENTS NEED LOVE AND REASSURANCE

The vast majority of patients whom a physician sees in the course of any given day are there because they do not love themselves properly. Many have a physical ailment, it is true, but, as one outstanding medical man told me, "Ninety-eight percent of the people who come to me would get well if they never saw a physician. They need reassurance, which is another name for love. Medication, pills, prescriptions, tests, and the loving concern that my staff and I give them are symbols of the love they need. And I do not deprecate their need and our response in the slightest."

One physician states that "pills are often substitutes for the time and personal attention the doctor cannot give. The more pills patients can get from their physician, the more they feel he cares for them. Refusing them medication really upsets them. They think we are withholding precious help out of lack of sympathy."

Another medical man stated that patients often seek hospitalization because, in that way, they can be certain of a daily visit from their physician and sympathy and attention from their family and friends.

Dr. Robert Baumler, writing in Physician's Management Journal, says, "Some hospital patients repeatedly flash the nursing desk to adjust a pillow, or a door opening, or curtains, as a way of making the nurse indicate T love you.' If a daughter can get a doctor out to see her old mother, particularly if he can be summoned immediately and somewhat imperiously, the parent will have to think the daughter loves her very much."

Let's face it: There are many millions of lonely people in the world. Some of them are surrounded by family and friends but are still lonely. It is a primal need for love that was never filled in childhood.

The event is in the past; the emotion is in the person, in the present. That is, the deprivation of love may have occurred in childhood thirty or fifty years ago, but the feeling —"I am not loved"—still resides in the individual. Such a person may go through life unaware of the unfulfilled need for love, conscious only of recurring illness, accidents, or of the fact that life is not working right. The message is: Love me, care for me, visit me, listen to me, meet my needs.

These people, of course, have little or no self-love. They do not consciously manipulate. They are not aware that they are devious and troublesome.

The child encapsulated within the adult is still sending the same message that began in the crib: "Notice me, listen to me, come touch me, hold me, cuddle me—let me know I am loved. I need you." Time does not diminish the ancient need. If anything, time intensifies it.

And as normal defenses and fulfillment diminish, the original need is felt more keenly. This is one reason older people sometimes become demanding and childish and unreasonable. They have come full circle. An aging person who received adequate love as a child, or who learned later the art of self-love, seldom becomes a crotchety, unirascible nuisance. Old age does not do anything for you except to make you more of what you are. What one was at thirty or fifty is simply intensified at seventy or ninety.

SELF-ESTEEM AND DEPRESSION

Let's take the matter of depression. There is a periodic or cyclical type of depression. Most people experience this to some degree from time to time, either as the result of accumulated stress or some disappointment or combination of factors.

Then there is the deep, all-encompassing type of depression that is almost beyond description. Life seems hopeless and useless. Death often seems preferable. Many people who attempt suicide are in the depths of this type of depression. There is a sense in which they are not "sane"; that is, they are not in full possession of all their faculties. The entire organism—physical, emotional, and spiritual—has been overloaded.

When a person is seriously depressed over an extended period of time, there is often some degree of malnutrition. The diet may be adequate by normal standards, but in depressed states, it is not just the mind that is undergoing depression; the entire system— mental, physical, and emotional—is '*down," functioning under par. Under severe emotional stress or depression, the body does not absorb vitamins and minerals as efficiently as under normal conditions.

Nothing can be more devastating to a person in deep depression than to be told to "snap out of it," "look on the bright side of things," "count your blessings," think how much worse off many people are." Another futile approach is to urge a depressed person to "have faith."

I recall a woman who, after her second cancer operation, went into a deep depression. Her well-meaning friends urged numerous cheery books upon her, offered vast amounts of advice, and sought to show her how to pray more effectively. Two of them assured her, as Job's "comforters" did that there must be some serious malfunction in her spiritual life. All were certain that if only she prayed hard enough, she could overcome the horrible depression that descended over her and enveloped her like a black cloud.

In a number of counseling sessions, I could discover no apparent reason for her depression, other than her deeply buried fear of death, intensified by her guilt-inducing friends.

I sent her to a psychiatrist-friend and told him there was no apparent reason for her depression other than fear and guilt over not being able to resolve the problem with prayer. After some experimentation, he found a combination of antidepressants and tranquilizers that met her needs. This was, as I told her, not a solution for the problem, but would handle the symptom. She rapidly regained her normally cheerful attitude, and we began to work on the problem of her false guilt and the understandable fear that had precipitated the crisis. In her depressed state, no form of talk therapy could reach her; but, relieved of the symptoms, she responded rapidly and, in a relatively short time, was able to dispense with the medication.

HEART ATTACKS, EMOTIONS, AND SELF-ESTEEM

It is now recognized that there is usually an emotional component in high blood pressure. This is also true in heart attacks. Drs. Friedman and Rosenman of San Francisco point out the factors that can contribute to a heart attack.^ If you tend to hurry someone with his speech by finishing his sentences for him; if you consistently do more than one thing at a time; if you are working on some problem while someone is talking to you; dictate letters to a secretary or a dictating machine while driving; or feel guilty if you are idle for a few days, or even for a few hours, you are Type A and are a good prospect for a heart attack. Type-B personalities, they claim, are less tense, more accepting, with a higher degree of tolerance for frustration.

Type-A personalities, they found, have an instantly aggressive response to trivial slights and threats. This, in turn, sets off a chain reaction of hormonal changes that can seriously impair the metabolism, with a resultant build-up of fats or cholesterol in the coronary arteries.

Some Type-A people may never have a heart attack, but their temperament may make them subject to other types of physical and/or emotional disasters. Type-A individuals are quick on the trigger, impatient, low intolerance for frustration. Why? Because they have not come to terms with life! Loving God, man, and oneself sufficiently gives one a different outlook on life. With enough of this kind of three-way love, one's entire personality changes. One develops a higher tolerance for frustration. He not only accepts himself better, but he can also accept others more readily, with all of their deficiencies. He is less bothered by irritants of all kinds—noise, delay, disappointment, threatening situations, fear of the future, death, or disaster.

You have seen people who "fight traffic." They cut in and out, jam on their brakes, push ahead, tense and anxious, irritated by other drivers, and end up at their destination often angry and half-exhausted.

Other drivers who may arrive thirty seconds to a few minutes later have been relaxed, flowing with traffic instead of fighting it. Traffic fighters usually are Type-A persons who fight life, the clock, and members of the family.

I am well aware of the fact that I manifest a few aspects of Type-A behavior, as does one of the authors of the book referred to. (He has had a heart attack, and has modified his behavior considerably.) I am not "wired" for a quiet, reflective, meditative life. So, by an act of will, working against a genetic and environmental tendency toward constant activity, I take myself by the back of the neck during the day and get myself into a reclining chair. I first turn off my telephone and close the door. This indicates that I am not available to anyone for any purpose. Fighting down the ancient "parent" tape that urges me to "keep busy, don't just sit there, run and get me the hammer," I put on the headphones and turn on the stereo. I listen to some quieting music, sometimes to a meditation tape. Occasionally I become so relaxed that I go to sleep for a few minutes.

We know in our heads that a daily quiet time leads to greater serenity. No one denies it. We recognize our need for meditation and prayer—to be alone and pull the tattered edges of our souls together. If this is so, then what perverse streak is it within us that causes us to cram each hour to overflowing with tasks that, if left undone, would not cause cosmic disaster?

I suggest that the answer is simple: We do not love ourselves. Because we don't, we gain some satisfaction and false self-esteem from working until we are gray-faced with fatigue, complaining the while about our busy schedules. At its core, it is substituting busyness for creativity and serenity.

<u>ARE YOU DRIVEN, OR DRIVING?</u>

"He restoreth my soul" was never said by anyone in a frantic race against time, panting and out of breath, guilt-ridden over not getting more done. I confess to feeling more virtuous when I have accomplished a great deal in a given day. I shall never completely erase my "parent tape." But I am muting it. As I write this, I have taken off two weeks—by an act of the will, because my schedule was full—to go and sit in a beautiful spot near Carmel, California, overlooking the Pacific. I can write, read, think, walk on the beach, photograph flowers, watch the breakers, write some more, prowl around Carmel, relax, read a mystery story, and still get in five to seven hours of writing a day.

It is a happy compromise I have made with my "driven self," the one that responds to the "parent tape," urging me to get in motion and not rest for a minute. I am fighting a moderately successful battle against what, for some strange reason, is called the Protestant Work Ethic. (I don't know many Buddhists who are compulsive workers, but I imagine numerous Catholics and any number of Jews, as well as atheists, are addicted.)

By way of emphasis, let's go over some of these important factors again:

People who practice the three-way love principle tend to have fewer physical and emotional problems. There is ample scientific evidence to validate this. More important, Jesus stressed this as the supreme principle, so it must have tremendous importance. Obeying this universal law is not something we do to make God happy. He's getting along fine. It is for our own well-being that we obey this injunction.

Those who experience this three-way love are less accident-prone. This has been observed by such psychiatrists as C. G. Jung and has been validated in human experience by many observers. When we love these cosmic principles instead of thinking of them as burdensome religious observances, we are eligible for the peace and serenity of which the psalmist speaks.

Proper self-love can help prevent heart attacks and illness. This is being validated by medical men in research conducted over a period of forty-five years. The organism was meant to function better when there is an absence of excessive stress. All of the organs undergo tension for which they were not designed when we drive ourselves too long and too hard.

We become more likable, more acceptable persons when we acquire self-esteem. Loving ourselves, we are less touchy, less prone to be judgmental, and more capable of deeper friendships. People may not know precisely what is wrong with us when we are filled with self-hate

Or a weak self-image, but they know something is wrong. They tend to relate to us more freely and openly when we like ourselves better.

The self-accepting person is far less likely to suffer depression. In a deep depression, there is usually some form of self-hate originating in the sense of loss, failure (or fear of failure), guilt, or some serious threat to the individual. One who practices the three-way love principle consistently has inner resources on which he can draw in a crisis.

Those with positive regard for themselves tend to flow with life instead of fighting it. They feel more in harmony with the universe, less out of synchronization. Life becomes less of a struggling, crushing, competitive game where someone always loses, and some may get hurt, and more of a pleasurable experience. In short, self-love is better for you in every way.

SELF-LOVE AND HEALTH

A young woman had been seeing me in private sessions for quite some time and was also in a therapy group. Her anxiety was almost unbelievable. She was able to hold down a job, but when the day was over, she was, as she expressed it, "a basket case." The group experience did not seem to help. Eventually, I said, "I want you to see a physician friend of mine for a six-hour glucose tolerance test. I think it probable that you have hypoglycemia" (low blood sugar). She resisted strongly until I refused to see her unless she would have the test. The results revealed that she was severely hypoglycemic. She was put on a low-blood-sugar diet (high protein, low carbohydrate). Within a few weeks, her excessive anxiety had vanished. She began to react normally. No one is able to say for sure whether emotional stress is the cause of the malfunctioning organism or whether it is the physical symptom that produces emotional distress. Perhaps it really doesn't matter.

Another young woman who I felt might have the same problem returned with the diagnosis of diabetes.

A middle-aged man with a very weak self-image went through several years of intensive therapy with half a dozen different therapists in an effort to get some relief; eventually, he had extensive In-Depth Therapy with significant results. However, there was still something missing. I sent him in for blood tests, specifying the test for hypoglycemia particularly. He, too, was suffering from low blood sugar. A month on the new diet did nothing for him. Then, after five weeks, he began to feel much better. To his great satisfaction, he eventually lost forty pounds, and his inner tension continued to lessen. What I am saying at this point is that there is no one simple solution. I wish there were. A thousand and one things can go wrong with the human organism, intensifying the result of an already weak self-image.

Sigmund Freud wrote to a friend in 1927: "I am firmly convinced that one day all these disturbances we are trying to understand will be treated by means of hormones or similar substances." This was before the discovery of vitamins and prior to the improvement of many modern medical techniques. Hopefully, in the next few decades, new medical discoveries will make possible the alleviation of many emotional and physical ailments that are so baffling at the present time.

HOW TO REBUILD YOUR SELF-ESTEEM

Here are the practical steps you can take to help you rebuild a better self-image.

Remember: Merely reading them will probably do you very little good. You will need to pick out one specific step at a time, write it on a card, and carry it with you.

Refer to it often during the week. Jot down on the card ways in which you can implement your goal. Carrying the card with you and looking at it frequently will activate your unconscious mind. Remember, as you begin, that there are no free lunches, no magic cures, no simple solutions for life-long problems. It took you all those years to become the person you are. It will take time to change your self-image.

I am not suggesting a palpitating, frenzied struggle, but a single-minded long-range program. Erich Fromm suggests that learning to love requires giving it a priority.

In the acquiring of an art, a disciplined effort is essential, whether it is learning to play the guitar, painting, or rear children; and diligent, disciplined effort is most often achieved alone. One may learn principles in a class, a church service, or a group, but one usually achieves competence in any art or skill by practicing it alone.

<u>SOME OF THE MEANS BY WHICH ONE ACHIEVES A PROPER SELF-ESTEEM:</u>

Accept emotionally, as well as intellectually, the idea that proper self-love is all right. Loving yourself properly is not egotism. Egotistical people actually dislike themselves intensely. Only those who accept and like themselves are capable of true humility. Such persons tend to view themselves with amused friendly tolerance. They are not engaged in a frantic, breathless campaign to win approval or praise. Since they accept themselves, they do not need the recognition of others to bolster their sense of identity.

Give up self-condemnation. Criticizing or condemning yourself generates more self-hate. It is just as wrong to keep up a constant barrage of self-criticism as it is to be critical of others; it is terribly destructive.

MOST SELF-HATE HAS ROOTS IN CHILDHOOD

One morning my wife served me coffee in bed. (To avoid charges of male chauvinism, I hasten to add that I sometimes do the same for her.) In a careless gesture, I upset the coffee over a bedside table, half a dozen books, the bed, and the rug. I had done the same thing once before. I exploded: "I hate myself when I do that!" With my wife's help, I mopped up the spilled coffee, dried off the books and papers, sponged off the rug, and leaned back to think about it. It was a minor event, but I suspected that there were some major emotions involved. Why should I hate myself for an occasional bit of clumsiness? As I let my mind roam back into the distant past, I could see a little boy at the dinner table, with a youngish mother, two older sisters, and father. I saw the child grasp a big glass of milk, lose control of it, and spill the contents all over the table. I could hear mother's "Oh, you spilled your milk!" (It seemed like a superfluous announcement.) I could sense the irritation and impatience with which the entire family went to work, mopping up the table.

I let myself relive that little kid's feeling. It was "I'm clumsy and stupid. They hate me." So now, I thought, all the rest of my life, I must beat them (parents, friends, family, whoever) to the punch, and before they can judge me as awkward or stupid, I must say it myself.

I smiled as I ran that film past my inner eye. So that was the source of the statement surprised out of me, 'T hate myself when I do that." It took only a few seconds to review that film, and another second or two to resolve never to say again, 'T hate me."

There had been a quick one-second flash, too, as the coffee spilled: "She (wife/mother) will be upset." But I realized instantly that my wife had never expressed the slightest irritation over minor accidents. After all, she is human and spills things too. So it was a mother, really, not my wife.

A small illustration that, but whether it be spilled

Coffee, or milk, or a moral lapse, one must learn to abandon self-hate. Review the incident and see how it can be avoided in the future. At that point, all remorse or guilt should subside.

<u>SHARING HELPS BUILD SELF-ESTEEM</u>

Join a sharing group. I am not referring to Bible study or prayer groups, good as these may be under proper leadership. I am recommending a group where honesty is encouraged, without attack, where advice is considered an insult, where others listen as you share your deepest needs or hurts or longings. In short, I am thinking of the kind of group where you are accepted as you are. Acceptance is an important aspect of love.

<u>DISTINGUISH BETWEEN NEUROTIC FANTASIES AND REALISTIC GOALS.</u>

Gladys, a married woman in her thirties, had a very rough childhood. She saw me weekly, and sometimes oftener, as she tried desperately to maintain her hold on sanity. She had so little self-worth that her self-hate emerged in the form of rage toward her husband and her eldest daughter. Partly as the result of her emotional instability, her husband lost his position, and the resultant financial crisis created more insecurity and anxiety in her. She was diagnosed as a paranoid schizophrenic.

During this period, Gladys shared many fantasies with me. She was confident that she could become a professional singer if she were only given a chance. She composed music and recorded it on tape, which she played for me. She was pathetically determined to "be somebody," to win applause and to be looked up to. Of course, I did not seek to dissuade her or to shatter her fantasies of glory. She needed them just then.

In time her paranoia diminished. The split halves of the self began to merge in a more solid fashion, and her fantasies lessened. She secured a job and appeared contented with what proved to be a fairly mundane position. Her dreams of glory vanished. She no longer needed them.

Frank's ambition illustrates a more realistic drive toward a goal that he ultimately reached. His sadistic, rejecting mother married a succession of five men. "All of them were bums," Frank said. In his early teens, he announced that he was going to be a football star at a great university and a millionaire by the time he was forty. His parents, of course, ridiculed his absurd boyish fantasies.

But he made his fantasy a reality! From some unexpected source, he drew strength and guidance. It never crossed his mind that he would fail to reach his goal. He did become a football star at a prestigious university. I knew him during the last ten years before he hit forty, for we spent considerable time working on his marriage. At forty, he had made his millions. He then resigned his position as president of the firm and began to look around for other fields of endeavor.

He wanted to do more than make money and would like to be involved in helping people.

There was a vast difference between Gladys' dream of glory and Frank's long-range goals. Gladys fantasized unrealistic attainments in order to compensate for terrifying feelings of self-hate; Frank set long-term goals toward which he worked consistently over a period of twenty-five years.

Most people find it necessary to scale down some of their childhood dreams of grandeur. Infantile megalomania, the early belief in one's omnipotence, gives way to reality. Only the individual can tell by trial and error, which is a good ambition and which is an unrealistic fantasy of glory.

MOTIVES: GOOD, BAD, AND MIXED

Check your motives. A college friend of mine once told me that his ambition was to make a lot of money and do a great deal of good in the world. Forty years later, he had done neither, though I expect that if he had not had mixed motives, he might have achieved one or the other of his goals.

The Taoist insight is pertinent: "*When the wrong man uses the right means, the right means work the wrong way.*" Ambition can be laudable, a proper means to an end, but the wrong man with dream may end up a failure.

"*The wrong man*" *is one whose motives are impaired. They are faulty if he is a manipulator if he is self-centered if he is punitive or seeks revenge if he is dishonest in pursuing even laudable goals if he lacks integrity if he seeks ease without labor.*

Since we all tend to conceal certain things from ourselves, it can be helpful to check your motives and goals with some objective person. Friends, not wanting to hurt us, may not always be honest. An emotionally uninvolved counselor, or a sharing group, will come closer to reflecting to you what they see and hear.

CHRISTIAN PERSPECTIVE FOR BUILDING SELF-ESTEEM

Do the things that will make you like yourself better. Jesus taught some universal principles that will work for Christian, Moslem, Jew, Buddhist, or atheist. A basic one is this: "Give, and it will be given to you . . ." (Luke 6:38, RSV). Give love, sympathy, help, understanding, forgiveness, money—whatever seems indicated. This "giving attitude" can involve a simple note of appreciation to a friend, giving undivided attention to someone who needs a listening ear, and without necessarily offering advice, pausing to talk to a child, a lonely person, or a frightened drop-out from society.

Jesus also said, "Give to him who begs from you, and do not refuse him who would borrow from you" (Matthew 5:42, RSV) and "Lend, expecting nothing in return" (Luke 6:35, RSV). When I lend a book, I hope to have it returned, usually a futile expectation. I would hesitate to estimate the number of my books now in the hands of other people.

The point of Jesus' teaching is this: He who lends and receives it back again has really done little if anything (Luke 6:34). It has cost him nothing; therefore, it is nothing to be proud of Bankers lend at interest and expect the loan to be repaid. That is their business. They do not claim any particular virtue for themselves as lenders. Nor should we, according to Jesus, think of it as a virtue if we lend and receive it back again. It becomes a virtue only if it is an open-handed gesture of love and concern with no strings.

Must we then allow ourselves to be taken advantage of by free-loaders, rip-off artists, and manipulators? I think not. Within our power, we are to do whatever is loving and helpful for people, but we are to use our God-given intelligence in deciding to whom and when to give or lend. It must not be done to buy their love and friendship, nor to purchase virtue, assuming that were possible.

"Give to him who asks of you." My feeling is that Jesus meant it to be taken seriously, not necessarily literally.

There are three possible responses to pleas for help. We can give people what they ask for; we can refuse to help; or we can discover the real need and try to meet it, within our capacity, on our own terms. This often takes much more time and skill than to grant the individual's request. But to seek out the real need is to express love, for love is not only an emotion or attitude, but it is also an action.

THINGS TO AVOID

Now we come to some of them do not. They are just as important as the positive steps:

Avoid name dropping.

This is one of the most used and abused ploys of people who are unsure of themselves. One who uses names of important people to bolster his sense of identity is broadcasting to the world that he has so little self-worth that he has to borrow the glitter and worth of others to add to his own shabby self-esteem. "As my friend, Joe was telling me the other day—he's the new mayor, you know. . . ." Reflected glory and borrowed fineries are one and the same. They belong to others.

Avoid negativism.

Some people with a weak self-image cannot think of constructive things to say, and settle for making negative or critical comments. I recall a man who, when his church was much smaller, held a position of some importance. As the membership grew, he was no longer a significant factor. At the conclusion of a lengthy board meeting, during which he had contributed nothing, he looked up at one of the chandeliers and said petulantly, "We'll just have to call the custodian's attention to the dead flies in these light fixtures. It looks terrible. He's not on the job." It was his only comment during a three-hour session.

Another board member with a negative attitude was noted for adding to any motion the warning: "Perhaps we should check into the legality of this matter before proceeding further." He seldom had anything else to offer. Perfectionistic, critical, petulant people are ultimately avoided.

Abstain from argumentativeness.

There are obviously times when one needs to stand up for a principle, or even for a method. That is different from being fundamentally argumentative. Self-rejecting people who have a measure of aggressiveness can often sound quarrelsome and petty.

I recall a brilliant and otherwise pleasant man of considerable ability who was gently persistent in committee and board meetings. In denominational meetings, he tended to bore in, gently, tactfully, but relentlessly, until everyone was bored and disgusted. He never learned the difference between a method and a principle. He would as readily spend an hour on some trivial process as on an important principle. He eventually lost his position, his influence, and his friends. He shared with me his deep conviction that he was being persecuted by his former friends. Paranoia had set in.

Postponement.

The road to neurosis, like the road to hell, is paved with good intentions, long postponed. You can delay, alibi, excuse, procrastinate, rationalize, and offer yourself a hundred reasons, but the only way to reach any worthwhile goal is to start. A great line of poetry has been turned into a cliche with a partial truth: "They also serve who only stand and wait"; but it is truer to state that they also starve who only stand and wait—starve for the good things of life: love and friendship and self-esteem.

Alcohol.

"The 'pleasure' of being drunk is obviously the pleasure of escaping from the responsibility of consciousness. And so are the kind of social gatherings, held for no other purpose than the expression of hysterical chaos, where the guests wander around in an alcoholic stupor, prattling noisily and senselessly, and enjoying the illusion of a universe where one is not burdened with purpose, logic, reality or awareness."

In the same category are **tranquilizers**, both uppers, and downers. There is a legitimate place for the temporary use of tranquilizers, but they do not provide a permanent solution for the nameless dread and anxiety lodged in the subterranean chambers of the personality. Frantic socialization. Those who cannot bear to be alone and must seek out companions in order to quiet the pathological anxiety originating in self-rejection are akin to the loners whose anxiety is intensified by social contact; both are seeking an escape from reality.

The geographical cure. This is a false solution sought by those who believe that a new job, or a new husband or wife, or a new house (clothes, car, trips, gadgets) will provide release from the ever-present anxiety being generated by low self-esteem.

Depression.

Most serious depression originates in self-hate and is an unconscious effort to shut off feelings. Depression is not an emotion, but results from the shutting down of feelings, to avoid feeling. The defense system, sometimes our friend but often our enemy, offers an illusionary escape from whatever feelings we would have to face otherwise.

Compulsive work. The compulsive worker is running from something. Sometimes it is an effort to avoid hearing an ancient "parent tape" accusing one of being lazy. Turning out a vast amount of work, refusing to take a vacation, bringing homework from the office, finding eighteen hours of work to do and never getting it finished—all these are efforts to win temporary respite from some muted but incessant voice that says, "You're no good unless you keep busy."

Compulsive sloth.

The compulsive worker can at least win temporary self-approval, and occasional admiration for the amount of work turned out, but the sloth gets only condemnation.
Whether it is the child staring dreamingly out of the school window, or the housewife slouched hour after hour before the television set (or the uncommunicative husband watching TV with a grunt, a grouch, and a can of beer),

or someone who is unmotivated and simply cannot get started, such a person confuses and antagonizes those of us who were taught that the devil has worked for idle hands. And if we happen to be diligent, hard-working, never-take-a-rest kind of persons, the lazy person challenges our sense of "oughtness." The truth is that the unmotivated or indolent individual is reacting to life in the only way he knows how at the moment. Accusations and admonitions worsen the situation. Intensive therapy is usually indicated.

Then there is the retreat into sickness, into excessive busyness, into bookishness, as with the professional student, and into a fantasy world, an escape from reality.

<u>GET INTO MOTION WITH A PRACTICAL COURSE OF ACTION.</u>

Let's look at some more of these possibilities:

Start paying compliments.

It will not be easy if you are unaccustomed to offering praise. Form the habit of noticing what people are wearing. If it is something new, a simple "Say, I like that!" will suffice. No one was ever insulted by a sincere compliment. Everyone wants to be noticed. If a friend has a new car or wins a promotion, you can either react with envy and wonder how he managed it, or say, "Congratulations on the new job," or car, or whatever.

In her widely syndicated column. Dear Abby replied to a woman who asked what kind of response one could give to a person who showed a picture of a child who was anything but attractive. Abby suggested that an appropriate response would be, '*You must be very proud." Good advice. A perfectly honest reply ("What an ugly child") would be devastating to the parent, but there is a higher law than honesty. It is the principle of love. The New Testament admonition about "speaking the truth in love" (Ephesians 4:15) is sound advice.

Psychologist William James pointed out that feelings follow actions. If you do not feel comfortable or sincere when you first start paying honest compliments, "act as if" you felt sincere, and in time you will not feel phony. Even if you do feel hypocritical at first, remember that it is never phony to act appropriately.

Give love and understanding.

You may feel lonely or depressed yourself, and it would be nice if someone visited you and expressed his love and concern. You may wait a long time. So begin at the giving point.

Through your church, your lodge, or office, find the names of shut-ins who are lonely and in need of regular visits. Whatever it is that you would like for others to do for you, do that for them, is the teaching of Jesus. You will not be doing it entirely for them; you will derive important benefits too. You will like yourself better. It is a wonderful way to build proper self-esteem.

I once knew a desperately depressed and lonely woman who had experienced ten years of emotional illness. Long before she had recovered sufficiently to hold down a job, she sought out two older women, members of her church, and visited them regularly. She spent hours listening, having occasional meals with them, and driving them places. The shut-ins were worse off than her, and she decided to give them love and attention. I counseled with her during part of her lengthy recovery and observed the therapeutic benefits of her program of visitation.

In most towns and cities, there are retirement and convalescent homes. Many of the people in these homes are terribly lonely. Some do not have a visitor from one month to the next. A phone call will provide the necessary information regarding visiting hours.

What if you don't really want to visit the lonely? If you don't feel like it, do it anyway! Remember that feelings follow actions. You're tired. You need attention; why should you be the one giving and loving when you need it as much as anyone else? Because it's good for you! You can wallow in your misery, or you can get into motion and feel better. The New Testament tells the story of ten lepers who approached Jesus for healing (Luke 17:12-19). He told them to go and show themselves to the priests for verification of their healing, which had not yet occurred. The account says, " four they went, they were cleansed" (v. 14, Kjv). You may not be healed of whatever it is that troubles you until you get into motion.

Begin the practice of forgiving yourself.

There are two aspects of forgiveness. One is God's forgiveness upon our confession and repentance. The other is existential forgiveness or the cleansing that takes place when at last, we are able to forgive ourselves. Most people have little difficulty believing that God forgives. The problem is in forgiving oneself.

The Prayer of Affirmation

The Twenty-third Psalm is a prayer of affirmation in which the psalmist affirms to his inner self what he knows intellectually about God. You can employ the same technique. Write this formula on a card and carry it with you indefinitely. Repeat it ten or a dozen times a day for three months. After you have reached your goal and are able to forgive yourself fully, the old feelings will probably return in time. It will not take as long the second time, nor the third or the fourth. Old habit patterns such as self-condemnation tend to reassert themselves but to a lesser degree.

Here is the formula:

I am neither good nor bad. I am both.

I am neither honest nor dishonest. I am both.

I am neither generous nor selfish. I am both.
(Make up your own list to fit your situation.)

But God accepts me, forgives me, and loves me, and

I now accept, forgive, and love myself

Learning to Be Quiet

Learn to meditate. (No magic, remember? Just a lot of hard work.) Meditation can be difficult, for it involves learning to be quiet, but most people who have tried daily meditation report new feelings of peace and serenity. Try two twenty-minute periods of meditation a day, or one thirty-minute session. (Two periods are better.)

Some people say that their minds wander when they meditate. But it is just a matter of practice and persistence.

There is another way to meditate. Take an inspirational book and read until you find something that stimulates your thinking. Stop right there. Shut the book, close your eyes, and ask yourself, "What would it involve if I were to apply that principle to my life?" Roll that question over in your mind until you have exhausted the possibilities. Then read again. It is important to stop immediately when you find a thought or principle that applies to you. To read beyond that point is "greedy reading," stuffing the mind with intellectual concepts without taking time to meditate on them and digest them emotionally.

Get Into Motion

Join an activity group. Every community has such groups. I recall a young man who was having serious difficulty in his marriage, which finally ended in divorce. I found him to be terribly immature. He seemed to lack ordinary common sense and consequently was in all manner of difficulty. He appeared to be a fairly hopeless cause. After the break-up of the marriage, I did not see him for two or three years.

The next time I saw him, he was emerging from the weekly meeting of the Toastmaster's Club, of which he had become an officer. I sensed a remarkable change in him. He was poised, relaxed, and friendly. It wasn't a put-on either; he was genuine. Since he had been learning to express himself, he had gained self-confidence. He had matured to a remarkable degree.

People need people.

We are gregarious beings who do not grow well in isolation. Some people who are very shy rationalize their sedentary habits with such generalizations as "People are shallow" or "I'd much rather read a good book."

The rationalizations may have an element of truth, but the fact remains that we tend to grow emotionally and spiritually "in community," working, worshiping, studying, and having fellowship with other people.

I recall two men with radically different approaches who united with the church, of which I was a senior minister. One was a diffident young man suffering from a serious inferiority complex. He had an outgoing, brilliant brother who had once been active as a leader among our young people. The shy brother joined and soon asked to be allowed to teach a class. He was definitely not teacher material. Sundry other opportunities were offered him, all of which he rejected. He was determined to be a teacher or nothing and eventually drifted away.

It is readily understandable that, with his monumental inferiority complex, he felt a need for a job with some prestige. (Abraham Lincoln was once approached by a man from his home state who asked to be appointed to a very important position. Lincoln said, *'That job requires a big man." The rather inadequate applicant replied, *'Mr. President, appoint me to the job, and I'll automatically be a big man.")

The other man who united with the church was a kindly physician, gentle, friendly, and unassuming. He said, "Dr. Osborne, I'm available for any job you have. Nothing is too small." The church hostess needed someone to help serve the food at the family-night dinners. He assented readily. And what a cheerful, effective disher-upper he was! He speeded up the waiting line by fifty percent over anyone else who had ever done the job. In the many years he belonged to the church, he served in a dozen or more capacities. Nothing was beneath him, and he proved capable in many major capacities as well.

Jesus said when observing how the Twelve jockeyed for position and prestige: "He who is greatest among you shall be your servant" (Matthew 23:11, Rsv). Humble service need not be humiliating, except to the person with a mammoth inferiority complex. At a church "clean-up" project, I watched a federal judge vigorously loading junk on a truck, and a society matron scrubbing the kitchen floor.

Listening Is an Act of Love

Learn to listen. Listening is an art, and few people acquire it. A good listener is rare, indeed. Listening with an abstracted air and glazed eyes are all too common. There are those who listen just long enough to find a suitable opening to interject their "Yes, and that reminds me of something that happened to me. ..."

Since listening is an act of love and of caring, it is surprising that so few people express loving concern in this way. Being a good listener is far more important than being a good talker. I am not suggesting the self-abasing attitude that

Says, "I'm nobody; I don't matter; don't pay any attention to me. I'm too timid to enter into the conversation, so I'll just listen." This wallflower type of passivity is not it at all. You are entitled to enter into the conversation. But the thing to be deplored in almost any group is the fact that so few people are actively listening. There is a big difference between listening actively and passively. The active listener may manifest interest by asking, *'Yes, and what happened then?" or by making some appropriate comment. Active listening involves three steps:

1. "What happened? Tell me about it."

2. Listen actively, encouraging the other to talk.

3. Validate the feeling, which calls for something like, "Yes, that was interesting. Your trip to Afghanistan sounds fascinating. I'd like to visit there sometime. Tell me more about it."

It isn't easy to affirm another person who has had a marvelous vacation in Tahiti, or experienced fabulous adventures in the Gobi desert, especially when envy is being felt in your every pore. But if you want to be a friend, you will want to practice active listening. It isn't easy to rejoice with a friend who has just bought a new Mercedes Benz; or who has had a fantastic promotion; or whose son has graduated summa cum laude from Harvard and has fabulous offers from IBM, and General Motors, But it is important to develop your sense of self-worth by learning to express interest and concern even when it is difficult.

Almost anyone can express love to the lovable, compassion to the down-trodden, and congratulations to a consistent loser who has finally achieved some minor goal. It is difficult to congratulate someone who may not deserve his good fortune or to listen to a bore when you would prefer to be almost anyplace else. It is in such circumstances as these that one builds self-esteem and acquires genuine self-love by practicing the loving art of listening.

Choose goals well within your reach.

Get-to-the-top-in-a-hurry syndrome has severe limitations. You may see people in some organizations who are chosen for significant positions of leadership or promotion who appear to have less ability than you. You can let it make you bitter and cynical, or you can stick it out. Your sterling qualities may not have been discovered yet.

In selecting goals, make sure that there is not too great a chance of failure. It is best to work toward goals that are readily attainable. Too many defeats can be disheartening and ultimately defeating.

And patience! (No magic, remember?) Any worthwhile achievement takes time. I once said to a group of ministers, "You have to be at least thirty, or married, to have learned that life is frustrating." A fine-looking young man in the front row said, "I'm twenty-nine, unmarried, and I'm already frustrated!" I replied, "You're to be congratulated. You're precocious."

In the selection of goals, it is important to avoid some common "defense-goals," that is, goals that are unconsciously utilized in an effort to achieve self-esteem but are really a futile defense against feelings of inferiority. These illustrate the principle:

The martyr-mother, who, having no genuine identity of her own, confuses her role as a mother with her identity. She has a sense of being "real" and worthwhile only as long as she can play the role of the ever-loving, always-sacrificing mother. She means well, but having no real self-love, she can derive a sense of false self-esteem by mothering her children, who by this time may be in their thirties or fifties. She is hurt when her unsolicited advice is ignored, and so she plays the martyr role. As she ages, she wants more and more attention from her children and may become utterly unreasonable with her increasing demands. Having sought self-worth by the mother's role, she knows no other way to achieve it.

— The "personality boy" who makes a career of being popular. He must be loved by everyone, for his self-worth is wrapped up not in who or what he is, but in the number of people who admire or love him. Such a man derives enormous satisfaction from his many feminine conquests. If he is rejected, he feels hurt and puzzled, for he has failed in his goal to win unconditional love (affirmation, sex, approval). His defense against seeing himself as he really is—self-doubting, unsure of himself—is to make certain that he is rejected as seldom as possible.

— The superachiever may have grown accustomed to constant adulation as a child because of good grades, superior talent, or ability to charm people. Not having known defeat, and being gifted in some way, such a person often confuses performance with the character and achievement with self-worth. One who seldom has if ever experienced failure or had to take second place often has difficulty accepting defeat graciously, and defeat, in this case, means not being looked up to and admired, or not being in the spotlight.

No One Ever Said It Would Be Easy Until maturity comes, many people tend to have the naive misconception that life is going to be easy. What a mistake! Life is very complex, and it can be disappointing and sometimes very lonely. Charles Darwin's theory of organic evolution rested heavily upon the concept of "the survival of the fittest." Some people imagine that this applies only to the animal world. It also includes humans. The records are full of countless species of plant and animal life that have died out because they didn't adapt. They were drop-outs in the battle for survival. And in the human struggle for survival, resilience and patient endurance are essential for survival.

Are you waiting for something wonderful to happen to you? There is always the remote possibility that it will. You could win the Irish sweepstakes; your daydreams could materialize; yes, the good fairy could appear and make it so. But it isn't likely, is it?

The statement of Jesus, perhaps not recorded in its entirety, goes like this: "Ask, and it will be given you; seek and you will find; knock and it will be opened to you" (Matthew 7:7, Rsv). At first, it sounds almost like magic, doesn't it? Yet the idea of magical answers to prayer is not consistent with the rest of his teachings. Let's make that read (as he may well have intended): "Ask and keep asking until you discover the answers; seek and keep on seeking until you find what it is you are looking for; don't give up! Knock on every door until you find the one that opens to you, and behind which there is something worthwhile."

Emotions, Health, and Self-Worth

Check your health. If you lack in drive and energy, it could be from physical as well as emotional causes: a malfunctioning thyroid, hypoglycemia (low blood sugar), a mineral imbalance, a vitamin deficiency, or a score of other causes.

At one point in my life, I experienced a significant loss of energy. I took all kinds of tests. One physician taught me to be a hypochondriac since excessive fatigue is one of the most common complaints in doctors' offices. Finally, insisting on more than a standard examination, I asked for exhaustive blood tests. The results came back, indicating four or five times the normal level of lead in my system. Just because you have had a physical examination and nothing serious was discovered doesn't mean that you are well physically. Sometimes more complete blood tests are needed.

Recent studies have shown that excessive coffee drinking can play a significant part in nervousness. People who are tense and nervous should limit their coffee intake and probably avoid it entirely, according to many authorities.

I recall a woman with severe emotional problems who did not respond to any form of therapy. Checking with her about her diet, I discovered that because of a neurotic fear of being obese like her mother, she had for years lived on a totally inadequate diet. I could not induce her to change it. No human organism could be expected to function well on her diet. Eventually, she ended up receiving shock therapy, preferring that to the threat of gaining weight. The results were minimal. She was, incidentally, at least twelve to fifteen pounds underweight.

Share your guilt.

This can be very threatening. Remember that time does not diminish guilt. The event may have transpired many years ago, but the sense of guilt remains unless you have a deep sense of having been forgiven and have forgiven yourself. I have dealt with people who have finally blurted out guilt feelings thirty and forty years old.

There was something self-defeating in the lives of each one. In one, there was a physical disability that defied medical science. In another, the woman kept getting fired, despite her great ability and brilliant mind. She was unconsciously punishing herself.

Shared Guilt Can Bring Relief

The longer some ancient guilt is kept concealed, the more damage it does to the personality, and the more terrible the guilt seems. Guilty secrets are very damaging to the personality and often account for continued defeat.

If you have a guilty secret, you can get relief by sharing it with an understanding, accepting minister, or with a psychologist or psychiatrist. Avoid, however, as you would, the plague, a counselor who is judgmental.

There is an understandable reluctance to share areas of guilt with another. One feels ashamed, embarrassed, and vulnerable. It often seems better, for the moment, to bury the guilt. The difficulty is that it requires a sizeable amount of psychic energy to keep up the pretense. Hiding buried guilt is stress-producing, and anyone in need of stronger self-acceptance needs all of the psychic energy he can summon. Learn to accept love, as well as give it. It can sometimes be less demeaning or embarrassing to give than to receive. It is humbling to be on the receiving end, to be in need, and seek help. To be a gracious recipient is as important as being a generous giver.

It is terrifying to be helpless, friendless, afraid, and ashamed. A woman was flung at Jesus' feet by the Pharisees, who were seeking to trap him (John 8:3-11). She had been caught in the very act of adultery, they said. (It is interesting that no charges were brought against the man.)

The law of Moses said that she should be stoned. Some in the crowd were already picking up stones for the exciting, self-righteous act of stoning the adulteress. It was a clever way of unconsciously dissipating their own guilt. "Let him who is without sin cast the first stone," Jesus said. Then he knelt and wrote in the sand with his finger. His face would have been on a level with hers.

"Let him who is without sin. . . ." There is an embarrassment, confusion, and dismay in the crowd. One by one, they begin to disperse. Don't look back. Look straight ahead. Urgent business elsewhere. Finally their ds no crowd left—just Jesus and a crouching woman.

"Where are your accusers?" She raises her head, looks about. "They've all gone." "Neither do I condemn you; you may go now—but—look, don't keep up this way of life, because if you do, you're going to hurt yourself." That's the sense and the spirit of what he said. But more important was that look. She would remember the words more clearly later when she relived the scene.

Just mow, she's looking into his eyes. They are warm and friendly and searching. They are forgiving eyes because there is love in them. No one had ever loved her this way before, and he is so relaxed, so accepting. He isn't judgemental. There's no indignation over her moral failure. She had condemned herself a hundred times, but the self-hate seemed to intensify the demand for some kind of affection, and the inner cry for someone to care—even for an hour or a night. Later, after she had left him, she would think again and again of the scene. "He protected me from those men.

They wanted to kill me! He saved me with a single sentence. I was so frightened; they were so hateful, so hideous. And some of those men I had known— intimately. And he—he was so tender, so gentle, yet strong, too.

"I will never forget those compassionate eyes. I think he liked me; no, it was more, he loved me, but in a way, I've never been loved before. How could he love me, after all, I've been? It isn't as if he didn't know. He knew! He knew without their having to tell him. He looked right into me and knew more than they could tell him. But he still liked me, accepted me, loved me— that's the amazing part. I don't know who he is, but I love him, in a way I've never loved anyone. I want to know him better. I'd even like to follow him, be with him. I wonder what it would be like just to be around him.

"And strange ... he made me like me better. I feel better about myself More—clean? Whole? Is that it? I feel that I could almost begin to love myself. Is this possible? He didn't condemn me. He accepted me, loved me—and now I can begin to love myself Beautiful!"

CONCLUSION

We are responsible for our individual lives. We have been imbued with a deep urge to express goodness and love, and have been granted "free will" and the immutable law of cause and effect to lead us into ever greater awareness—so that we can free ourselves of ignorance and self-imposed bondage—so that we can each become a whole person, a serene, self-loving individual who truly "loves his neighbor as himself." What we do with our lives is up to each of us, whether we live in "fear and trembling," in self-loathing and misery, or whether we embark on an even more exciting and rewarding adventure, free of false and distorted concepts, conflict, futility, and frustration, of the inhibiting and debilitating emotional turmoil of crippling self-esteem.

In sum, we will achieve sound self-esteem to the degree that we realize the following: that we each have the sole responsibility, the authority, freedom, and ability to direct our own lives and affairs as we see fit; that people are innately "good," worthy and important, nonphysical essences, unique and precious beings; and that at our divine center each of us is inviolable, invincible and eternal; that no matter how badly we may err, how much we may stumble or slip backward in our tortuous upward climb, we are each an inseparable part of a Common Source, varying only in our awareness; that regardless how slow and uneven the rate, we are each ever-growing in wisdom and love; and that we have all the time there is for our unfoldment—and that all our experience is but a means to this end.

The acid test for a truly high self-esteem is this:

Do you, when you occasionally happen to focus your awareness on yourself, spontaneously experience a subtle surge of warmth and love, as you do perhaps when you pause to think lovingly of your sweetheart, spouse, or child?

If you do, however, fleeting this sense of warmth and love toward yourself maybe, you are one of those rare individuals who has a genuine appreciation and regard for your own intrinsic worth.

Blank Page

BIBLIOGRAPHY

^Frederick Leboyer, *Birth Without Violence* (New York: Alfred A. Knopf, 1975).

^Erich Fromm, *The Art of Loving* (New York: Harper and Row, 1956).

B. Watson, *Psychological Care of Infant and Child* (New York: Norton & Co., 1928).

^Nathaniel Branden, *The Psychology of Self-Esteem* (New York: Bantam Books, 1975).

^William A. Miller, *Why Do Christians Break Down?* (Minneapolis: Augsburg Publishing House, 1973).

^Nathaniel Branden, *The Psychology of Self-Esteem* (New York: Bantam Books, 1975).

^*San Francisco Chronicle*, September 16, 1975. ^ ^,. ^.

^Associated with Yokefellows, Inc., 19 Park Road, Burlingame, CA 94010.

^Meyer Friedman, MD, and Ray Rosenman, MD, *Type A Behavior and Your Heart* (New York: Fawcett Publications, 1975).

^Karl Menninger, *Love Against Hate* (New York: Harcourt Brace Jovanovich, 1959).

^Sigmund Freud, *Dictionary of Psychoanalysis* (New York: Fawcett Publications, n.d.), with a preface by Theodore Reik.

^Sigmund Freud, *Dictionary of Psychoanalysis* (New York: Fawcett Publications, n.d.), with a preface by Theodore Reik.

^Meyer Friedman, MD, and Ray Rosenman, MD, *Type A Behavior and Your Heart* (New York: Fawcett Publications, 1975).